LAB MANUAL

VISTAS

Introducción a la lengua española

SECOND EDITION

Blanco • Donley

VISTA
HIGHER LEARNING

Boston, Massachusetts

ISBN 1-59334-368-X

4 5 6 7 8 9 DBH 09 08 07 06 05

Table of Contents

Introduction

The VISTAS Lab Manual

Completely coordinated with the **VISTAS** student textbook, the Lab Manual for **VISTAS** provides you with additional practice of the vocabulary, grammar, and language functions presented in each of the textbook's eighteen lessons. The Lab Manual will also help you to continue building your listening and speaking skills in Spanish. Icons and page references in the **recursos** boxes of the **VISTAS** student textbook correlate the Lab Manual to your textbook, letting you know when activities are available for use. Answers to the Lab Manual activities are located in a separate Answer Key. Additionally, the **recursos** boxes in the **VISTAS 2/e** Lab Manual correlate the activities to the Lab CDs and the MP3 Files Audio CD-ROM.

The laboratory activities are designed for use with the **VISTAS** Lab CDs or MP3 Files Audio CD-ROM. They focus on building your listening comprehension, speaking, and pronunciation skills in Spanish, as they reinforce the vocabulary and grammar of the corresponding textbook lesson. The lab manual guides you through the Lab CDs/MP3 files, providing the written cues—direction lines, models, charts, drawings, etc.—you will need in order to follow along easily. You will hear statements, questions, mini-dialogues, conversations, monologues, commercials, and many other kinds of listening passages, all recorded by native Spanish speakers. You will encounter a wide range of activities, such as listening-and-repeating exercises, listening-and-speaking practice, listening-and-writing activities, illustration-based work, and dictations.

Each laboratory lesson contains a **Contextos** section that practices the active vocabulary taught in the corresponding textbook lesson. In **Lecciones 1–9**, a **Pronunciación** section follows; it parallels the one found in your textbook, and, in addition, offers a dictation exercise. In **Lecciones 10–18**, the **Pronunciación** sections are unique to the Lab Manual and the Lab CDs/MP3 files since, in those lessons, your textbook features **Ortografía** sections instead of **Pronunciación**. Each laboratory lesson then concludes with an **Estructura** section and closes with a **Vocabulario** section that allows you to listen to and repeat the active vocabulary listed on the final page of the corresponding section in the student textbook.

We hope that you will find the **VISTAS** Lab Manual to be a useful language learning resource and that it will help you to increase your Spanish language skills in a productive, enjoyable fashion.

*The **VISTAS** Authors and the Vista Higher Learning Editorial Staff*

contextos

Lección 1

1 Identificar You will hear six short exchanges. For each one, decide whether it is a greeting, an introduction, or a leave-taking. Mark the appropriate column with an **X.**

> **modelo**
>
> *You hear:* RAQUEL David, te presento a Paulina.
>   DAVID Encantado.
> *You mark:* an **X** under *Introduction.*

	Greeting	Introduction	Leave-taking
Modelo	_____	X _____	_____
1.	_____	_____	_____
2.	_____	_____	_____
3.	_____	_____	_____
4.	_____	_____	_____
5.	_____	_____	_____
6.	_____	_____	_____

2 Asociar You will hear three conversations. Look at the drawing and write the number of the conversation under the appropriate group of people.

a. _____   b. _____   c. _____

3 Preguntas Listen to each question or statement and respond with an answer from the list in your lab manual. Repeat the correct response after the speaker.

a. Mucho gusto.

b. Chau.

c. Nada.

d. Lo siento.

e. Bien, gracias.

f. Soy de los Estados Unidos.

pronunciación

The Spanish alphabet

The Spanish alphabet consisted of 30 letters until 1994, when the **Real Academia Española** (Royal Spanish Academy) removed **ch (che)** and **ll (elle)**. You may see **ch** and **ll** listed as separate letters in reference works printed before 1994. Two Spanish letters, **ñ (eñe)** and **rr (erre)**, don't appear in the English alphabet. The letters **k (ka)** and **w (doble ve)** are used only in words of foreign origin.

Letra	Nombre(s)	Ejemplo(s)	Letra	Nombre(s)	Ejemplo(s)
a	a	**a**diós	ñ	eñe	ma**ñ**ana
b	be	**b**ien, pro**b**lema	o	o	**o**nce
c	ce	**c**osa, **c**ero	p	pe	**p**rofesor
d	de	**d**iario, na**d**a	q	cu	**q**ué
e	e	**e**studiante	r	ere	**r**egular, seño**r**a
f	efe	**f**oto	rr	erre	ca**rr**o
g	ge	**g**racias, **G**erardo, re**g**ular	s	ese	**s**eñor
h	hache	**h**ola	t	te	**t**ú
i	i	**i**gualmente	u	u	**u**sted
j	jota	**J**avier	v	ve	**v**ista, nue**v**o
k	ka, ca	**k**ilómetro	w	doble ve	*walkman*
l	ele	**l**ápiz	x	equis	e**x**istir, Mé**x**ico
m	eme	**m**apa	y	i griega, ye	**y**o
n	ene	**n**acionalidad	z	zeta, ceta	**z**ona

1 **El alfabeto** Repeat the Spanish alphabet and example words after the speaker.

2 **Práctica** When you hear the number, say the corresponding word aloud and then spell it. Then listen to the speaker and repeat the correct response.

1. nada
2. maleta
3. quince
4. muy
5. hombre
6. por favor
7. San Fernando
8. Estados Unidos
9. Puerto Rico
10. España
11. Javier
12. Ecuador
13. Maite
14. gracias
15. Nueva York

3 **Dictado** You will hear six people introduce themselves. Listen carefully and write the people's names as they spell them.

1. _____
2. _____
3. _____
4. _____
5. _____
6. _____

recurso

Lab CDs/MP3s
Lección 1

estructura

1.1 Nouns and articles

1   **Identificar** You will hear a series of words. Decide whether the word is masculine or feminine, and mark an **X** in the appropriate column.

> **modelo**
>
> *You hear:* lección
> *You mark:* an **X** under *feminine.*

	Masculine	Feminine
Modelo	_____	X
1.	_____	_____
2.	_____	_____
3.	_____	_____
4.	_____	_____
5.	_____	_____
6.	_____	_____
7.	_____	_____
8.	_____	_____

2   **Transformar** Change each word from the masculine to the feminine. Repeat the correct answer after the speaker. (*6 items*)

> **modelo**
>
> el chico
> la *chica*

3   **Cambiar** Change each word from the singular to the plural. Repeat the correct answer after the speaker. (*8 items*)

> **modelo**
>
> una palabra
> unas palabras

4   **Completar** Listen as Silvia reads her shopping list. Write the missing words in your lab manual.

_____ diccionario
un _____
_____ cuadernos
_____ grabadora
_____ mapa (map) de _____
_____ lápices

1.2 Numbers 0–30

1 **Bingo** You are going to play two games (*juegos*) of bingo. As you hear each number, mark it with an **X** on your bingo card.

Juego 1		
1	3	5
29	25	6
14	18	17
9	12	21

Juego 2		
0	30	27
10	3	2
16	19	4
28	22	20

2 **Números** Use the cue in your lab manual to tell how many there are of each item. Repeat the correct response after the speaker.

> **modelo**
> You see: 18 chicos
> You say: dieciocho chicos

1. 15 lápices
2. 4 computadoras
3. 8 cuadernos
4. 22 días
5. 9 grabadoras
6. 30 fotos
7. 1 palabra
8. 26 diccionarios
9. 12 países
10. 3 problemas
11. 17 escuelas
12. 25 turistas

3 **Completar** You will hear a series of math problems. Write the missing numbers and solve the problems.

1. _____ + _____ = _____
2. _____ − _____ = _____
3. _____ + _____ = _____
4. _____ − _____ = _____
5. _____ + _____ = _____
6. _____ + _____ = _____

4 **Preguntas** Look at the drawing and answer each question you hear. Repeat the correct response after the speaker. (*6 items*)

1.3 Present tense of ser

1   **Identificar**   Listen to each sentence and mark an **X** in the column for the subject of the verb.

> **modelo**
> *You hear:* Son pasajeros.
> *You mark:* an **X** under **ellos.**

	yo	tú	él	nosotros	ellos
Modelo	____	____	____	____	X ____
1.	____	____	____	____	____
2.	____	____	____	____	____
3.	____	____	____	____	____
4.	____	____	____	____	____
5.	____	____	____	____	____
6.	____	____	____	____	____

2   **Cambiar**   Form a new sentence using the cue you hear as the subject. Repeat the correct answer after the speaker. (*8 items*)

> **modelo**
> Isabel es de los Estados Unidos. (yo)
> *Yo soy de los Estados Unidos.*

3   **Escoger**   Listen to each question and choose the most logical response.

1. a. Soy Patricia.   b. Es la señora Gómez.
2. a. Es de California.   b. Él es conductor.
3. a. Es del Ecuador.   b. Es un diccionario.
4. a. Es de Patricia.   b. Soy estudiante.
5. a. Él es conductor.   b. Es de España.
6. a. Es un cuaderno.   b. Soy de los Estados Unidos.

4   **Preguntas**   Answer each question you hear using the cue in your lab manual. Repeat the correct response after the speaker.

> **modelo**
> *You hear:* ¿De dónde es Pablo?
> *You see:* Estados Unidos
> *You say:* Él es de los Estados Unidos.

1. España   2. California   3. México   4. Ecuador   5. Puerto Rico   6. Colorado

5   **¿Quiénes son?**   Listen to this conversation and write the answers to the questions in your lab manual.

1. ¿Cómo se llama el hombre? _____
2. ¿Cómo se llama la mujer? _____
3. ¿De dónde es él? _____
4. ¿De dónde es ella? _____
5. ¿Quién es estudiante? _____
6. ¿Quién es profesor? _____

1.4 Telling time

1 **La hora** Look at the clock and listen to the statement. Indicate whether the statement is **cierto** or **falso**.

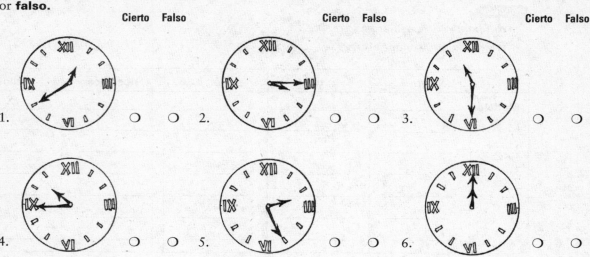

Cierto   Falso   Cierto   Falso   Cierto   Falso

1.   ○   ○   2.   ○   ○   3.   ○   ○

4.   ○   ○   5.   ○   ○   6.   ○   ○

2 **Preguntas** Some people want to know what time it is. Answer their questions, using the cues in your lab manual. Repeat the correct response after the speaker.

> **modelo**
> *You hear:* ¿Qué hora es, por favor?
> *You see:* 3:10 p.m.
> *You say:* Son las tres y diez de la tarde.

1. 1:30 P.M.   3. 2:05 P.M.   5. 4:54 P.M.

2. 9:06 A.M.   4. 7:15 A.M.   6. 10:23 P.M.

3 **¿A qué hora?** You are trying to plan your class schedule. Ask your counselor what time these classes meet and write the answer.

> **modelo**
> *You see:* la clase de economía
> *You say:* ¿A qué hora es la clase de economía?
> *You hear:* Es a las once y veinte de la mañana.
> *You write:* 11:20 A.M.

1. la clase de biología: _____   4. la clase de literatura: _____

2. la clase de arte: _____   5. la clase de historia: _____

3. la clase de matemáticas: _____   6. la clase de sociología: _____

vocabulario

You will now hear the vocabulary for **Lección 1** found on page 34 of your textbook. Listen and repeat each Spanish word or phrase after the speaker.

contextos

Lección 2

1 Identificar Look at each drawing and listen to the statement. Indicate whether the statement is **cierto** or **falso**.

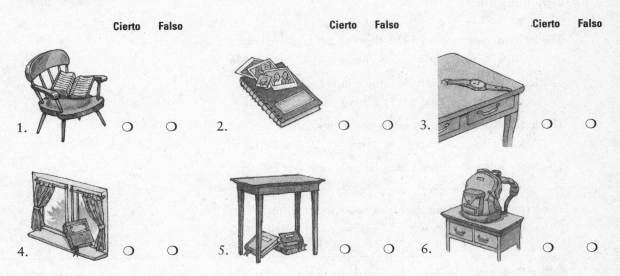

2 ¿Qué día es? Your friend Diego is never sure what day of the week it is. Respond to his questions, saying that it is the day before the one he mentions. Then repeat the correct answer after the speaker. (6 *items*)

> **modelo**
> Hoy es domingo, ¿no?
> No, hoy es sábado.

3 Preguntas You will hear a series of questions. Look at Susana's schedule for today and answer each question. Then repeat the correct response after the speaker.

Martes 18

9:00 economía — Sr. Rivera

11:00 química —Sra. Hernández

12:15 cafetería—Carmen

1:30 prueba de contabilidad — Sr. Ramos

3:00 matemáticas — Srta. Torres

4:30 laboratorio de computación — Héctor

recurso
Lab CDs/MP3s
Lección 2

pronunciación

Spanish vowels

Spanish vowels are never silent; they are always pronounced in a short, crisp way without the glide sounds used in English.

a   **e**   **i**   **o**   **u**

The letter **a** is pronounced like the a in *father*, but shorter.

Álex   cl**a**se   n**a**d**a**   enc**a**nt**a**d**a**

The letter **e** is pronounced like the e in *they*, but shorter.

el   **e**n**e**   m**e**sa   **e**l**e**fant**e**

The letter **i** sounds like the ee in *beet*, but shorter.

Inés   ch**i**ca   t**i**za   señor**i**ta

The letter **o** is pronounced like the o in *tone*, but shorter.

h**o**la   c**o**n   libr**o**   d**o**n Francisc**o**

The letter **u** sounds like the oo in *room*, but shorter.

uno   reg**u**lar   sal**u**dos   g**u**sto

---

1 **Práctica** Practice the vowels by repeating the names of these places in Spain after the speaker.

1. Madrid   5. Barcelona
2. Alicante   6. Granada
3. Tenerife   7. Burgos
4. Toledo   8. La Coruña

---

2 **Oraciones** Repeat each sentence after the speaker, focusing on the vowels.

1. Hola. Me llamo Ramiro Morgado.
2. Estudio arte en la Universidad de Salamanca.
3. Tomo también literatura y contabilidad.
4. Ay, tengo clase en cinco minutos. ¡Nos vemos!

---

3 **Refranes** Repeat each saying after the speaker to practice vowels.

1. Del dicho al hecho hay un gran trecho.
2. Cada loco con su tema.

---

4 **Dictado** You will hear a conversation. Listen carefully and write what you hear during the pauses. The entire conversation will then be repeated so you can check your work.

JUAN _____

_____

_____

ROSA _____

JUAN _____

ROSA _____

recurso
Lab CDs/MP3s
Lección 2

estructura

2.1 Present tense of **-ar** verbs

1 **Identificar** Listen to each sentence and mark an **X** in the column for the subject of the verb.

> *modelo*
> *You hear:* Trabajo en la cafetería.
> *You mark:* an **X** under **yo**.

	yo	tú	él	nosotros	ellos
Modelo	X				
1.					
2.					
3.					
4.					
5.					
6.					
7.					
8.					

2 **Cambiar** Form a new sentence using the cue you hear as the subject. Repeat the correct answer after the speaker. (*6 items*)

> *modelo*
> María practica los verbos ahora. (José y María)
> *José y María practican los verbos ahora.*

3 **Preguntas** Answer each question you hear in the negative. Repeat the correct response after the speaker. (*8 items*)

> *modelo*
> ¿Estudias geografía?
> *No, yo no estudio geografía.*

4 **Completar** Listen to the following description and write the missing words in your lab manual.

Teresa y yo (1) _____ en la Universidad Autónoma de Madrid. Teresa

(2) _____ lenguas extranjeras. Ella (3) _____ trabajar en

las Naciones Unidas (*United Nations*). Yo (4) _____ clases de periodismo.

También me gusta (5) _____ y (6) _____. Los sábados

(7) _____ con una tuna. Una tuna es una orquesta (*orchestra*) estudiantil.

Los jóvenes de la tuna (8) _____ por las calles (*streets*) y

(9) _____ canciones (*songs*) tradicionales de España.

2.2 Forming questions in Spanish

1 **Escoger** Listen to each question and choose the most logical response.

1. a. Porque mañana es la prueba.   b. Porque no hay clase mañana.
2. a. Viaja en autobús.   b. Viaja a Toledo.
3. a. Llegamos a las cuatro y media.   b. Llegamos al estadio.
4. a. Isabel y Diego dibujan.   b. Dibujan en la clase de arte.
5. a. No, enseña física.   b. No, enseña en la Universidad Politécnica.
6. a. Escuchan la grabadora.   b. Escuchan música clásica.
7. a. Sí, me gusta mucho.   b. Miro la televisión en la residencia.
8. a. Hay diccionarios en la biblioteca. b. Hay tres.

2 **Cambiar** Change each sentence into a question using the cue in your lab manual. Repeat the correct response after the speaker.

> **modelo**
>
> *You hear:* Los turistas toman el autobús.
> *You see:* ¿Quiénes?
> *You say:* ¿Quiénes toman el autobús?

1. ¿Dónde?   3. ¿Qué?   5. ¿Cuándo?   7. ¿Quiénes?
2. ¿Cuántos?   4. ¿Quién?   6. ¿Dónde?   8. ¿Qué?

3 **¿Lógico o ilógico?** You will hear some questions and the responses. Decide if they are **lógico** (*logical*) or **ilógico** (*illogical*).

1. Lógico   Ilógico   3. Lógico   Ilógico   5. Lógico   Ilógico
2. Lógico   Ilógico   4. Lógico   Ilógico   6. Lógico   Ilógico

4 **Un anuncio** Listen to this radio advertisement and answer the questions in your lab manual.

1. ¿Dónde está (*is*) la Escuela Cervantes? _____

_____

2. ¿Qué cursos ofrecen (*do they offer*) en la Escuela Cervantes? _____

_____

3. ¿Cuándo practican los estudiantes el español? _____

_____

4. ¿Adónde viajan los estudiantes de la Escuela Cervantes? _____

_____

2.3 Present tense of **estar**

1 **Describir** Look at the drawing and listen to each statement. Indicate whether the statement is **cierto** or **falso**.

	Cierto	Falso			Cierto	Falso			Cierto	Falso			Cierto	Falso
1.	○	○		3.	○	○		5.	○	○		7.	○	○
2.	○	○		4.	○	○		6.	○	○		8.	○	○

2 **Cambiar** Form a new sentence using the cue you hear. Repeat the correct answer after the speaker. (*8 items*)

> *modelo*
> Irma está en la biblioteca. (Irma y Hugo)
> Irma y Hugo están en la biblioteca.

3 **Escoger** You will hear some sentences with a beep in place of the verb. Decide which form of **ser** or **estar** should complete each sentence and circle it.

> *modelo*
> *You hear:* Javier *(beep)* estudiante.
> *You circle:* **es** because the sentence is *Javier es estudiante.*

1. es	está	5. es	está
2. es	está	6. eres	estás
3. es	está	7. son	están
4. Somos	Estamos	8. Son	Están

2.4 Numbers 31–100

1 **Números de teléfono** You want to invite some classmates to a party, but you don't have their telephone numbers. Ask the person who sits beside you what their telephone numbers are, and write the answer.

> **modelo**
>
> *You see:* Elián
> *You say:* ¿Cuál es el número de teléfono de Elián?
> *You hear:* Es el ocho, cuarenta y tres, cero, ocho, treinta y cinco.
> *You write:* 843-0835

1. Arturo: _____   5. Simón: _____

2. Alicia : _____   6. Eva: _____

3. Roberto: _____   7. José Antonio: _____

4. Graciela: _____   8. Mariana: _____

2 **Preguntas** You and a coworker are taking inventory at the university bookstore. Answer your coworker's questions using the cues in your lab manual. Repeat the correct response after the speaker.

> **modelo**
>
> *You hear:* ¿Cuántos diccionarios hay?
> *You see:* 45
> *You say:* Hay cuarenta y cinco diccionarios.

1. 56	3. 64	5. 95	7. 31
2. 32	4. 83	6. 48	8. 79

3 **Mensaje telefónico** Listen to this telephone conversation and complete the phone message in your lab manual with the correct information.

Mensaje telefónico

Para (*For*) _____

De parte de (*From*) _____

Teléfono _____

Mensaje _____

_____

_____

_____

---

vocabulario

You will now hear the vocabulary for **Lección 2** found on page 68 of your textbook. Listen and repeat each Spanish word or phrase after the speaker.

contextos

Lección 3

1 **Escoger** You will hear some questions. Look at the family tree and choose the correct answer to each question.

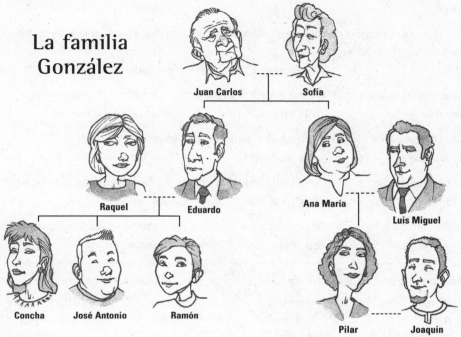

La familia González

Juan Carlos — Sofía

Raquel — Eduardo   Ana María — Luis Miguel

Concha   José Antonio   Ramón

Pilar — Joaquín

1. a. Pilar   b. Concha   5. a. José Antonio y Ramón   b. Eduardo y Ana María
2. a. Luis Miguel   b. Eduardo   6. a. Joaquín   b. Eduardo
3. a. Sofía   b. Ana María   7. a. Ana María   b. Sofía
4. a. Raquel   b. Sofía   8. a. Luis Miguel   b. Juan Carlos

2 **La familia González** Héctor wants to verify the relationship between various members of the González family. Look at the drawing and answer his questions with the correct information. Repeat the correct response after the speaker. (*6 items*)

> **modelo**
> Juan Carlos es el abuelo de Eduardo, ¿verdad?
> No, Juan Carlos es el padre de Eduardo.

3 **Profesiones** Listen to each statement and write the number of the statement below the drawing it describes.

a. _____   b. _____   c. _____   d. _____

recurso
Lab CDs/MP3s
Lección 3

pronunciación

Diphthongs and linking

In Spanish, **a, e,** and **o** are considered strong vowels. The weak vowels are **i** and **u.**

hermano   niña   cuñado

A diphthong is a combination of two weak vowels or of a strong vowel and a weak vowel. Diphthongs are pronounced as a single syllable.

ruido   pa**rie**ntes   pe**rio**dista

Two identical vowel sounds that appear together are pronounced like one long vowel.

la abuela   mi **hi**jo   una clas**e e**xcelente

Two identical consonants together sound like a single consonant.

con **N**atalia   su**s s**obrinos   la**s s**illas

A consonant at the end of a word is always linked with the vowel sound at the beginning of the next word.

E**s i**ngeniera.   mi**s a**buelos   su**s h**ijos

A vowel at the end of a word is always linked with the vowel sound at the beginning of the next word.

mi **h**ermano   su **e**sposa   nuestr**o a**migo

---

1 **Práctica** Repeat each word after the speaker, focusing on the diphthongs.

1. historia	4. novia	7. puerta	10. estudiar
2. nieto	5. residencia	8. ciencias	11. izquierda
3. parientes	6. prueba	9. lenguas	12. ecuatoriano

---

2 **Oraciones** When you hear the number, read the corresponding sentence aloud. Then listen to the speaker and repeat the sentence.

1. Hola. Me llamo Anita Amaral. Soy del Ecuador.
2. Somos seis en mi familia.
3. Tengo dos hermanos y una hermana.
4. Mi papá es del Ecuador y mi mamá es de España.

---

3 **Refranes** Repeat each saying after the speaker to practice diphthongs and linking sounds.

1. Cuando una puerta se cierra, otra se abre.
2. Hablando del rey de Roma, por la puerta se asoma.

---

4 **Dictado** You will hear eight sentences. Each will be said twice. Listen carefully and write what you hear.

1. _____
2. _____
3. _____
4. _____
5. _____
6. _____
7. _____
8. _____

estructura

3.1 Descriptive adjectives

1 **Transformar** Change each sentence from the masculine to the feminine. Repeat the correct answer after the speaker. (*6 items*)

> **modelo**
> El chico es mexicano.
> La *chica es mexicana.*

2 **Cambiar** Change each sentence from the singular to the plural. Repeat the correct answer after the speaker.

> **modelo**
> El profesor es ecuatoriano.
> Los *profesores son ecuatorianos.*

3 **Mis compañeros de clase** Describe your classmates, using the cues in your lab manual. Repeat the correct response after the speaker.

> **modelo**
> You hear: María
> You see: alto
> You say: María *es alta.*

1. simpático
2. rubio
3. inteligente
4. pelirrojo y muy bonito

5. alto y moreno
6. delgado y trabajador
7. bajo y gordo
8. tonto

4 **Completar** Listen to the following description and write the missing words in your lab manual.

Mañana mis parientes llegan de Guayaquil. Son cinco personas: mi abuela Isabel, tío Carlos y tía

Josefina y mis primos Susana y Tomás. Mi primaz es (1)_____ y (2)_____

. Baila muy bien. Tomás es un niño (3)_____, pero es (4)_____. Tío

Carlos es (5)_____ y (6)_____. Tía Josefina es (7)_____ y

(8)_____. Mi abuela es (9)_____ y muy (10)_____.

5 **La familia Rivas** Look at the photo of the Rivas family and listen to each statement. Indicate whether the statement is **cierto** or **falso**.

	Cierto	Falso
1.	○	○
2.	○	○
3.	○	○
4.	○	○

	Cierto	Falso
5.	○	○
6.	○	○
7.	○	○

3.2 Possessive adjectives

1 **Identificar** Listen to each statement and mark an **X** in the column for the possessive adjective you hear.

> **modelo**
> *You hear:* Es mi diccionario de español.
> *You mark:* an **X** under *my.*

	my	*your* (familiar)	*your* (formal)	*his/her*	*our*	*their*
Modelo	X					
1.						
2.						
3.						
4.						
5.						
6.						
7.						
8.						

2 **Escoger** Listen to each question and choose the most logical response.

1. a. No, su hijastro no está aquí.
   b. Sí, tu hijastro está aquí.
2. a. No, nuestros abuelos son canadienses.
   b. Sí, sus abuelos son norteamericanos.
3. a. Sí, tu hijo trabaja ahora.
   b. Sí, mi hijo trabaja en la librería Goya.
4. a. Sus padres regresan a las nueve.
   b. Mis padres regresan a las nueve.
5. a. Nuestra hermana se llama Margarita.
   b. Su hermana se llama Margarita.
6. a. Tus plumas están en el escritorio.
   b. Sus plumas están en el escritorio.
7. a. No, mi sobrino es ingeniero.
   b. Sí, nuestro sobrino es programador.
8. a. Su horario es muy bueno.
   b. Nuestro horario es muy bueno.

3 **Preguntas** Answer each question you hear in the affirmative using the appropriate possessive adjective. Repeat the correct response after the speaker. (*7 items*)

> **modelo**
> ¿Es tu lápiz?
> Sí, *es mi lápiz.*

3.3 Present tense of **-er** and **-ir** verbs

1 **Identificar** Listen to each statement and mark an **X** in the column for the subject of the verb.

> *modelo*
> *You hear:* Corro con Dora mañana.
> *You mark:* an **X** under **yo**.

	yo	tú	él	nosotros	ellos
Modelo	X				
1.					
2.					
3.					
4.					
5.					
6.					

2 **Cambiar** Listen to the following statements. Using the cues you hear, say that these people do the same activities. Repeat the correct answer after the speaker. (*8 items*)

> *modelo*
> Julia aprende francés. (mi amigo)
> **Mi amigo también aprende francés.**

3 **Preguntas** Answer each question you hear in the negative. Repeat the correct response after the speaker. (*8 items*)

> *modelo*
> ¿Viven ellos en una residencia estudiantil?
> **No, ellos no viven en una residencia estudiantil.**

4 **Describir** Listen to each statement and write the number of the statement below the drawing it describes.

a. _____ b. _____ c. _____ d. _____

3.4 Present tense of **tener** and **venir**

1 **Cambiar** Form a new sentence using the cue you hear as the subject. Repeat the correct answer after the speaker. (6 *items*)

> *modelo*
> Alicia viene a las seis. (David y Rita)
> **David y Rita vienen a las seis.**

2 **Consejos (*Advice*)** Some people are not doing what they should. Say what they have to do. Repeat the correct response after the speaker. (6 *items*)

> *modelo*
> Elena no trabaja.
> **Elena tiene que trabajar.**

3 **Preguntas** Answer each question you hear using the cue in your lab manual. Repeat the correct answer after the speaker.

> *modelo*
> ¿Tienen sueño los niños? (no)
> **No, los niños no tienen sueño.**

1. sí   3. no   5. sí   7. el domingo
2. Roberto   4. dos   6. mis tíos

4 **Situaciones** Listen to each situation and choose the appropriate **tener** expression. Each situation will be repeated.

1. a. Tienes sueño.   b. Tienes prisa.
2. a. Tienen mucho cuidado.   b. Tienen hambre.
3. a. Tenemos mucho calor.   b. Tenemos mucho frío.
4. a. Tengo sed.   b. Tengo hambre.
5. a. Ella tiene razón.   b. Ella no tiene razón.
6. a. Tengo miedo.   b. Tengo sueño.

5 **Mi familia** Listen to the following description. Then read the statements in your lab manual and decide whether they are **cierto** or **falso**.

	Cierto	Falso		Cierto	Falso
1. Francisco desea ser periodista.	○	○	4. Él tiene una familia pequeña.	○	○
2. Francisco tiene 20 años.	○	○	5. Su madre es inglesa.	○	○
3. Francisco vive con su familia.	○	○	6. Francisco tiene una hermana mayor.	○	○

vocabulario

You will now hear the vocabulary for **Lección 3** found on page 102 of your textbook. Listen and repeat each Spanish word or phrase after the speaker.

contextos

Lección 4

1 Lugares

Lugares You will hear six people describe what they are doing. Choose the place that corresponds to the activity.

1. _____

2. _____

3. _____

4. _____

5. _____

6. _____

a. el museo

b. el café

c. la piscina

d. el cine

e. el estadio

f. las montañas

g. el parque

h. la biblioteca

2 Describir

Describir For each drawing, you will hear two statements. Choose the one that corresponds to the drawing.

1. a.   b.

2. a.   b.

3. a.   b.

4. a.   b.

3 Completar

Completar Listen to this description and write the missing words in your lab manual.

Chapultepec es un (1) _____ muy grande en el (2) _____ de

la (3) _____ de México. Los (4) _____ muchas

(5) _____ llegan a Chapultepec a pasear, descansar y practicar

(6) _____ como (*like*) el (7) _____ , el fútbol, el vóleibol y

el (8) _____ . Muchos turistas también (9) _____ por

Chapultepec. Visitan los (10) _____ y el (11) _____ a los

Niños Héroes.

recurso
Lab CDs/MP3s
Lección 4

pronunciación

Word stress and accent marks

Every Spanish syllable contains at least one vowel. When two vowels are joined in the same syllable, they form a diphthong. A monosyllable is a word formed by a single syllable.

pe - lí - cu - la   e - di - fi - cio   ver   yo

The syllable of a Spanish word that is pronounced most emphatically is the "stressed" syllable.

bi - blio - **te** - ca   vi - si - **tar**   **par** - que   **fút** - bol

Words that end in **n**, **s**, or a vowel are usually stressed on the next to last syllable.

pe - **lo** - ta   pis - **ci** - na   **ra**- tos   **ha** - blan

If words that end in **n**, **s**, or a vowel are stressed on the last syllable, they must carry an accent mark on the stressed syllable.

na - ta - **ción**   pa - **pá**   in - **glés**   Jo - **sé**

Words that do not end in **n**, **s**, or a vowel are usually stressed on the last syllable.

bai - **lar**   es - pa - **ñol**   u - ni - ver - si - **dad**   tra - ba - ja - **dor**

If words that do not end in **n**, **s**, or a vowel are stressed on the next to last syllable, they must carry an accent mark on the stressed syllable.

béis - bol   **lá** - piz   **ár** - bol   **Gó** - mez

---

1 **Práctica** Repeat each word after the speaker, stressing the correct syllable.

1. profesor   4. Mazatlán   7. niños   10. México
2. Puebla   5. examen   8. Guadalajara   11. están
3. ¿Cuántos?   6. ¿Cómo?   9. programador   12. geografía

---

2 **Conversación** Repeat the conversation after the speaker to practice word stress.

MARINA   Hola, Carlos. ¿Qué tal?
CARLOS   Bien. Oye, ¿a qué hora es el partido de fútbol?
MARINA   Creo que es a las siete.
CARLOS   ¿Quieres ir?
MARINA   Lo siento, pero no puedo. Tengo que estudiar biología.

---

3 **Refranes** Repeat each saying after the speaker to practice word stress.

1. Quien ríe de último, ríe mejor.   2. En la unión está la fuerza.

---

4 **Dictado** You will hear six sentences. Each will be said twice. Listen carefully and write what you hear.

1. _____
2. _____
3. _____
4. _____
5. _____
6. _____

estructura

4.1 Present tense of **ir**

1 **Identificar** Listen to each sentence and mark an **X** in the column for the subject of the verb you hear.

> **modelo**
> *You hear:* Van a ver una película.
> *You mark:* an **X** under **ellos**.

	yo	tú	él	nosotros	ellos
Modelo	_____	_____	_____	_____	X
1.	_____	_____	_____	_____	_____
2.	_____	_____	_____	_____	_____
3.	_____	_____	_____	_____	_____
4.	_____	_____	_____	_____	_____
5.	_____	_____	_____	_____	_____
6.	_____	_____	_____	_____	_____

2 **Cambiar** Form a new sentence using the cue you hear as the subject. Repeat the correct answer after the speaker. (*8 items*)

> **modelo**
> Ustedes van al Museo Frida Kahlo. (yo)
> Yo voy al Museo Frida Kahlo.

3 **Preguntas** Answer each question you hear using the cue in your lab manual. Repeat the correct response after the speaker.

> **modelo**
> *You hear:* ¿Quiénes van a la piscina?
> *You see:* Gustavo y Elisa
> *You say:* Gustavo y Elisa van a la piscina.

1. mis amigos
2. en el Café Tacuba
3. al partido de baloncesto
4. no
5. sí
6. pasear en bicicleta

4 **¡Vamos!** Listen to this conversation. Then read the statements in your lab manual and decide whether they are **cierto** or **falso**.

	Cierto	Falso
1. Claudia va a ir al gimnasio.	○	○
2. Claudia necesita comprar una mochila.	○	○
3. Sergio va a visitar a su tía.	○	○
4. Sergio va al gimnasio a las ocho de la noche.	○	○
5. Sergio va a ir al cine a las seis.	○	○
6. Claudia y Sergio van a ver una película.	○	○

4.2 Stem-changing verbs: e→ie, o→ue

1 **Identificar** Listen to each sentence and write the infinitive form of the verb you hear.

> **modelo**
> *You hear:* No entiendo el problema.
> *You write:* entender

1. _____   4. _____   7. _____

2. _____   5. _____   8. _____

3. _____   6. _____

2 **Preguntas** Answer each question you hear using the cue in your lab manual. Repeat the correct response after the speaker.

> **modelo**
> *You hear:* ¿A qué hora comienza el partido?
> *You see:* 2:15 p.m.
> *You say:* El partido comienza a las dos y cuarto de la tarde.

1. el jueves   3. sí   5. leer una revista   7. a las tres
2. no   4. sí   6. mirar la televisión   8. Samuel

3 **Diversiones** Look at these listings from the entertainment section in a newspaper. Then listen to the questions and write the answers.

23D

MÚSICA	Pinturas de José Clemente Orozco	Campeonato de baloncesto
Palacio de Bellas Artes	De martes a domingo,	Los Universitarios vs. Los Toros
Ballet folklórico	de 10:00 a.m. a 6:00 p.m.	Gimnasio Municipal
Viernes 9, 8:30 p.m.	Entrada libre	Sábado 10, 7:30 p.m.
Bosque de Chapultepec	**DEPORTES**	**Torneo de Golf**
Concierto de música mexicana	**Copa Internacional de Fútbol**	con Lee Treviño
Domingo, 1:00 p.m.	México vs. Guatemala	Club de Golf Atlas
MUSEOS	Estadio Martín	Domingo 8, 9:00 a.m.
Museo de Arte Moderno	Viernes 9, 8:30 p.m.	

1. _____

2. _____

3. _____

4. _____

5. _____

4.3 Stem-changing verbs: e→i

1 Completar Listen to this radio broadcast and fill in the missing words.

Este fin de semana los excursionistas (1)_____ por más senderos *(trails)*. Dicen

que ir de (2)_____ a las montañas es una (3)_____ muy

popular y (4)_____ que (5)_____ más senderos. Si lo

(6)_____, la gente va a (7)_____ muy feliz. Si no, ustedes

pueden (8)_____ la historia aquí, en Radio Montaña.

2 Escoger Listen to each question and choose the most logical response.

1. a. Normalmente pido tacos.   b. Voy al restaurante los lunes.
2. a. Consigo novelas en la biblioteca.   b. Compro revistas en el centro.
3. a. Repiten la película el sábado.   b. No deseo verla.
4. a. Sigue un programa de baloncesto.   b. No, está buceando.
5. a. Nunca pido pizza.   b. Nunca pido perdón.
6. a. Prefiere visitar un monumento.   b. Prefiere buscarla en la biblioteca.
7. a. ¿Quién fue el primer presidente?   b. A las cuatro de la tarde.
8. a. ¡Sí, son muy interesantes!   b. Sí, mi hermano juega.

3 Conversación Listen to the conversation and answer the questions.

1. ¿Qué quiere Paola?

_____

2. ¿Por qué repite Paola las palabras?

_____

3. ¿Hace Miguel el favor que le pide Paola?

_____

4. ¿Dónde puede conseguir la revista?

_____

4.4 Verbs with irregular **yo** forms

1   **Describir**   For each drawing, you will hear two statements. Choose the one that corresponds to the drawing.

1. a. _____   b. _____

2. a. _____   b. _____

3. a. _____   b. _____

4. a. _____   b. _____

2   **Yo también**   Listen to the following statements about Roberto and respond by saying that you do the same things. Repeat the correct answer after the speaker. (*5 items*)

> **modelo**
>
> Roberto siempre *(always)* hace ejercicio *(exercise)*.
> Yo también hago ejercicio.

3   **Completar**   Listen to this telephone conversation and complete the statements.

1. Cristina ve _____.

2. Manuel y Ricardo quieren ir al parque para _____.

3. Manuel y Ricardo _____ las pelotas.

4. Manuel _____ la hora porque Cristina no _____.

5. Los chicos salen para el parque _____.

vocabulario

You will now hear the vocabulary found in your textbook on the last page of this lesson. Listen and repeat each Spanish word or phrase after the speaker.

contextos

Lección 5

1 **Identificar** You will hear a series of words. Write the word that does not belong in each series.

1. _____ 5. _____

2. _____ 6. _____

3. _____ 7. _____

4. _____ 8. _____

2 **Describir** For each drawing, you will hear two statements. Choose the one that corresponds to the drawing.

1. a.   b.   2. a.   b.   3. a.   b.

3 **En la agencia de viajes** Listen to this conversation between Mr. Vega and a travel agent. Then read the statements in your lab manual and decide whether they are **cierto** or **falso**.

	Cierto	Falso
1. El Sr. Vega quiere esquiar, pescar y hacer turismo.	○	○
2. El Sr. Vega va a hacer una excursión a Puerto Rico.	○	○
3. El Sr. Vega quiere ir de vacaciones la primera semana de mayo.	○	○
4. Una habitación en Las Tres Palmas cuesta (*costs*) $85.00.	○	○
5. El hotel tiene restaurante, piscina y jacuzzi.	○	○

4 **Escoger** Listen to each statement and choose the most appropriate activity for that weather condition.

1. a. Vamos a ir a la piscina.   b. Vamos a poner la televisión.

2. a. Voy a escribir una carta.   b. Voy a bucear.

3. a. Vamos al parque.   b. Vamos a tomar el sol.

4. a. Mañana voy a pasear en bicicleta.   b. Mañana voy a esquiar.

5. a. Queremos ir al cine.   b. Queremos nadar.

6. a. Voy a correr en el parque.   b. Voy a leer un libro.

7. a. Quiero escuchar música.   b. Quiero jugar al golf.

pronunciación

Spanish **b** and **v**

There is no difference in pronunciation between the Spanish letters **b** and **v**. However, each letter can be pronounced two different ways, depending on which letters appear next to them.

| **b**ueno | **v**ólei**b**ol | **b**i**b**lioteca | **v**i**v**ir |

B and **v** are pronounced like the English hard **b** when they appear either as the first letter of a word, at the beginning of a phrase, or after **m** or **n**.

| **b**onito | **v**iajar | tam**b**ién | in**v**estigar |

In all other positions, **b** and **v** have a softer pronunciation, which has no equivalent in English. Unlike the hard **b**, which is produced by tightly closing the lips and stopping the flow of air, the soft **b** is produced by keeping the lips slightly open.

| de**b**er | no**v**io | a**b**ril | cer**v**eza |

In both pronunciations, there is no difference in sound between **b** and **v**. The English **v** sound, produced by friction between the upper teeth and lower lip, does not exist in Spanish. Instead, the soft **b** comes from friction between the two lips.

| **b**ola | **v**ela | Cari**b**e | decli**v**e |

When **b** or **v** begins a word, its pronunciation depends on the previous word. At the beginning of a phrase or after a word that ends in **m** or **n**, it is pronounced as a hard **b**.

Verónica y su esposo cantan ‿**b**oleros.

Words that begin with **b** or **v** are pronounced with a soft **b** if they appear immediately after a word that ends in a vowel or any consonant other than **m** or **n**.

Benito es de ‿**B**oquerón pero ‿**v**ive en ‿**V**ictoria.

---

1 **Práctica** Repeat these words after the speaker to practice the **b** and the **v**.

1. hablamos	4. van	7. doble	10. cabaña
2. trabajar	5. contabilidad	8. novia	11. llave
3. botones	6. bien	9. béisbol	12. invierno

---

2 **Oraciones** When you hear the number, read the corresponding sentence aloud, focusing on the **b** and **v** sounds. Then listen to the speaker and repeat the sentence.

1. Vamos a Guaynabo en autobús.
2. Voy de vacaciones a la isla Culebra.
3. Tengo una habitación individual en el octavo piso.
4. Víctor y Eva van por avión al Caribe.
5. La planta baja es bonita también.
6. ¿Qué vamos a ver en Bayamón?
7. Beatriz, la novia de Víctor, es de Arecibo, Puerto Rico.

---

3 **Refranes** Repeat each saying after the speaker to practice the **b** and the **v**.

1. No hay mal que por bien no venga.
2. Hombre prevenido vale por dos.

---

4 **Dictado** You will hear four sentences. Each will be said twice. Listen carefully and write what you hear.

1. _____
2. _____
3. _____
4. _____

estructura

5.1 Estar with conditions and emotions

1 **Describir** For each drawing, you will hear two statements. Choose the one that corresponds to the drawing.

1. a. _____   b. _____   2. a. _____   b. _____

3. a. _____   b. _____   4. a. _____   b. _____

2 **Cambiar** Form a new sentence using the cue you hear as the subject. Repeat the correct answer after the speaker. (*5 items*)

> modelo
>
> Rubén está enojado con Patricia. (mamá)
> **Mamá *está enojada con Patricia.***

3 **Preguntas** Answer each question you hear using the cues in your lab manual. Repeat the correct response after the speaker.

> modelo
>
> *You hear:* ¿Está triste Tomás?
> *You see:* no / contento/a
> *You say:* **No, Tomás está contento.**

1. no / abierto/a   3. su hermano   5. no / sucio/a
2. sí   4. no / ordenado/a   6. estar de vacaciones

4 **Situaciones** You will hear four brief conversations. Choose the statement that expresses how the people feel in each situation.

1. a. Ricardo está nervioso.   b. Ricardo está cansado.
2. a. La señora Fuentes está contenta.   b. La señora Fuentes está preocupada.
3. a. Eugenio está aburrido.   b. Eugenio está avergonzado.
4. a. Rosario y Alonso están equivocados. b. Rosario y Alonso están enojados.

5.2 The present progressive

1 **Escoger** Listen to what these people are doing. Then read the statements in your lab manual and choose the appropriate description.

1. a. Es profesor.   b. Es estudiante.
2. a. Es botones.   b. Es inspector de aduanas.
3. a. Eres artista.   b. Eres huésped.
4. a. Son jugadoras de fútbol.   b. Son programadoras.
5. a. Es ingeniero.   b. Es botones.
6. a. Son turistas.   b. Son empleados.

2 **Transformar** Change each sentence from the present tense to the present progressive. Repeat the correct answer after the speaker. (*6 items*)

> modelo
>
> Adriana confirma su reservación.
> Adriana **está confirmando** su reservación.

3 **Preguntas** Answer each question you hear using the cue in your lab manual and the present progressive. Repeat the correct response after the speaker.

> modelo
>
> *You hear:* ¿Qué hacen ellos?
> *You see:* jugar a las cartas
> *You say:* Ellos **están jugando** a las cartas.

1. hacer las maletas   3. dormir   5. hablar con el botones
2. pescar en el mar   4. correr en el parque   6. comer en el café

4 **Describir** You will hear some questions. Look at the drawing and respond to each question. Repeat the correct answer after the speaker. (*6 items*)

5.3 Ser and estar

1 **Escoger** You will hear some questions with a beep in place of the verb. Decide which form of **ser** or **estar** should complete each question and circle it.

> **modelo**
> *You hear:* ¿Cómo (beep)?
> *You circle:* **estás** because the question is **¿Cómo estás?**

1. es	está	4. Es	Está
2. Son	Están	5. Es	Está
3. Es	Está	6. Es	Está

2 **¿Cómo es?** You just met Rosa Beltrán at a party. Describe her to a friend by using **ser** or **estar** with the cues you hear. Repeat the correct response after the speaker. (*6 items*)

> **modelo**
> muy amable
> *Rosa es muy amable.*

3 **¿Ser o estar?** You will hear the subject of a sentence. Complete the sentence using a form of **ser** or **estar** and the cue in your lab manual. Repeat the correct response after the speaker.

> **modelo**
> *You hear:* Papá
> *You see:* en San Juan
> *You say:* Papá está en San Juan.

| 1. inspector de aduanas | 3. a las diez | 5. el 14 de febrero |
| 2. la estación del tren | 4. ocupados | 6. corriendo a clase |

4 **¿Lógico o no?** You will hear some statements. Decide if they are **lógico** or **ilógico**.

1. Lógico	Ilógico	4. Lógico	Ilógico
2. Lógico	Ilógico	5. Lógico	Ilógico
3. Lógico	Ilógico	6. Lógico	Ilógico

5 **Ponce** Listen to Carolina's description of her vacation and answer the questions in your lab manual.

1. ¿Dónde está Ponce?

_____

2. ¿Qué tiempo está haciendo?

_____

3. ¿Qué es el Parque de Bombas?

_____

4. ¿Que día es hoy?

_____

5. ¿Por qué no va Carolina al Parque de Bombas hoy?

_____

5.4 Direct object nouns and pronouns

1 **Escoger** Listen to each question and choose the most logical response.

1. a. Sí, voy a comprarlo.
   b. No, no voy a comprarla.

2. a. Joaquín lo tiene.
   b. Joaquín la tiene.

3. a. Sí, los puedo llevar.
   b. No, no te puedo llevar.

4. a. Irene los tiene.
   b. Irene las tiene.

5. a. Sí, te llevamos al partido.
   b. Sí, nos llevas al partido.

6. a. No, vamos a hacerlo mañana.
   b. No, vamos a hacerla mañana.

7. a. Va a conseguirlos mañana.
   b. Va a conseguirlas mañana.

8. a. Pienso visitarla el fin de semana.
   b. Pienso visitarte el fin de semana.

2 **Cambiar** Restate each sentence you hear using a direct object pronoun. Repeat the correct answer after the speaker. (6 *items*)

> modelo
> Isabel está mirando la televisión.
> Isabel está mirándola.

Isabel está mirando la televisión... con Diego.

3 **No veo nada** You just broke your glasses and now you can't see anything. Respond to each statement using a direct object pronoun. Repeat the correct answer after the speaker. (6 *items*)

> modelo
> Allí está el Museo de Arte e Historia.
> ¿Dónde? No lo veo.

4 **Preguntas** Answer each question you hear in the negative. Repeat the correct response after the speaker. (6 *items*)

> modelo
> ¿Haces la excursión a El Yunque?
> No, no la hago.

vocabulario

You will now hear the vocabulary for **Lección 5** found on page 168 of your textbook. Listen and repeat each Spanish word or phrase after the speaker.

contextos

Lección 6

1 **¿Lógico o ilógico?** Listen to each statement and indicate if it is **lógico** or **ilógico**.

1. Lógico   Ilógico   5. Lógico   Ilógico
2. Lógico   Ilógico   6. Lógico   Ilógico
3. Lógico   Ilógico   7. Lógico   Ilógico
4. Lógico   Ilógico   8. Lógico   Ilógico

2 **Escoger** Listen as each person talks about the clothing he or she needs to buy, then choose the activity for which the clothing would be appropriate.

1. a. ir a la playa   b. ir al cine
2. a. jugar al golf   b. buscar trabajo (*work*)
3. a. salir a bailar   b. ir a las montañas
4. a. montar a caballo   b. jugar a las cartas
5. a. jugar al voleibol   b. comer en un restaurante elegante
6. a. hacer un viaje   b. patinar en línea

3 **Preguntas** Respond to each question saying that the opposite is true. Repeat the correct answer after the speaker. (*6 items*)

> modelo
> Las sandalias cuestan mucho, ¿no?
> No, las sandalias cuestan poco.

4 **Describir** You will hear some questions. Look at the drawing and write the answer to each question.

Diana   Carmen

1. _____
2. _____
3. _____
4. _____

pronunciación

The consonants **d** and **t**

Like **b** and **v**, the Spanish **d** can have a hard sound or a soft sound, depending on which letters appear next to it.

¿**D**ónde?	ven**d**er	na**d**ar	ver**d**a**d**

At the beginning of a phrase and after **n** or **l**, the letter **d** is pronounced with a hard sound. This sound is similar to the English *d* in *dog*, but a little softer and duller. The tongue should touch the back of the upper teeth, not the roof of the mouth.

Don	**d**inero	tien**d**a	fal**d**a

In all other positions, **d** has a soft sound. It is similar to the English *th* in *there*, but a little softer.

me**d**ias	ver**d**e	vesti**d**o	huéspe**d**

When **d** begins a word, its pronunciation depends on the previous word. At the beginning of a phrase or after a word that ends in **n** or **l**, it is pronounced as a hard **d**.

Don **D**iego no tiene el **d**iccionario.

Words that begin with **d** are pronounced with a soft **d** if they appear immediately after a word that ends in a vowel or any consonant other than **n** or **l**.

Doña **D**olores es **d**e la capital.

When pronouncing the Spanish **t**, the tongue should touch the back of the upper teeth, not the roof of the mouth. In contrast to the English *t*, no air is expelled from the mouth.

traje	pan**t**alones	**t**arje**t**a	**t**ienda

---

1 **Práctica** Repeat each phrase after the speaker to practice the **d** and the **t**.

1. Hasta pronto.
2. De nada.
3. Mucho gusto.
4. Lo siento.
5. No hay de qué.
6. ¿De dónde es usted?
7. ¡Todos a bordo!
8. No puedo.
9. Es estupendo.
10. No tengo computadora.
11. ¿Cuándo vienen?
12. Son las tres y media.

---

2 **Oraciones** When you hear the number, read the corresponding sentence aloud, focusing on the **d** and **t** sounds. Then listen to the speaker and repeat the sentence.

1. Don Teodoro tiene una tienda en un almacén en La Habana.
2. Don Teodoro vende muchos trajes, vestidos y zapatos todos los días.
3. Un día un turista, Federico Machado, entra en la tienda para comprar un par de botas.
4. Federico regatea con don Teodoro y compra las botas y también un par de sandalias.

---

3 **Refranes** Repeat each saying after the speaker to practice the **d** and the **t**.

1. En la variedad está el gusto.
2. Aunque la mona se vista de seda, mona se queda.

---

4 **Dictado** You will hear four sentences. Each will be said twice. Listen carefully and write what you hear.

1. _____
2. _____
3. _____
4. _____

estructura

6.1 Numbers 101 and higher

1 **Poblaciones** Look at the population figures in the chart and listen to each statement. Then indicate whether the statement is **cierto** or **falso**.

País	Población
Argentina	37.944.000
Chile	15.589.000
Colombia	43.821.000
Cuba	11.275.000
Ecuador	13.112.000
España	39.584.000
Guatemala	11.995.000
México	101.851.000
Perú	26.523.000
Puerto Rico	3.930.000

	Cierto	Falso
1.	○	○
2.	○	○
3.	○	○
4.	○	○
5.	○	○
6.	○	○

2 **Dictado** Listen carefully and write each number as numerals rather than words.

1. _____   4. _____   7. _____

2. _____   5. _____   8. _____

3. _____   6. _____   9. _____

3 **Preguntas** Answer each question you hear using the cue in your lab manual. Repeat the correct response after the speaker.

> **modelo**
> *You hear:* ¿Cuántas personas hay en Chile?
> *You see:* 15.589.000
> *You say:* Hay quince millones, quinientas ochenta y nueve mil personas en Chile.

1. 800   3. 1284   5. 172

2. 356   4. 711   6. unos 43.000

4 **Un anuncio** Listen to this radio advertisement and write the prices for each item listed in your lab manual. Then figure out what the total cost for the trip would be.

Pasaje de avión: _____

Barco: _____

Total para las tres excursiones: _____

6.2 Indirect object pronouns

1 **Escoger** Listen to each question and choose the most logical response.

1. a. Sí, le mostré el abrigo.

   b. Sí, me mostró el abrigo.

2. a. No, no le presté el suéter azul.

   b. No, no te prestó el suéter azul.

3. a. Voy a comprarles ropa interior.

   b. Vamos a comprarle ropa interior.

4. a. Sí, nos dieron las nuevas sandalias.

   b. Sí, me dieron las nuevas sandalias.

5. a. Nos costaron veinte dólares.

   b. Les costaron veinte dólares.

6. a. Sí, nos traigo un sombrero.

   b. Sí, te traigo un sombrero.

2 **Transformar** Cecilia has been shopping. Say for whom she bought these items using indirect object pronouns. Repeat the correct answer after the speaker. (6 *items*)

> **modelo**
> Cecilia compró una bolsa para Dora.
> *Cecilia le compró una bolsa.*

3 **Preguntas** Answer each question you hear using the cue in your lab manual. Repeat the correct response after the speaker.

> **modelo**
> *You hear:* ¿Quién está esperándote?
> *You see:* Mauricio
> *You say:* Mauricio *está esperándome.*

1. sí   3. no   5. Antonio
2. $50,00   4. su traje nuevo   6. bluejeans

4 **En el centro comercial** Listen to this conversation and answer the questions in your lab manual.

1. ¿Quién es Gustavo?

   _____

2. ¿Qué está haciendo Gustavo?

   _____

3. ¿Qué le preguntó Gustavo a José?

   _____

4. ¿Por qué le prestó dinero José?

   _____

5. ¿Cuándo va a regalarle (*to give*) la falda a Norma?

   _____

6.3 Preterite tense of regular verbs

1 **Identificar** Listen to each sentence and decide whether the verb is in the present or the preterite tense. Mark an **X** in the appropriate column.

> *modelo*
> You hear: Alejandro llevó un suéter marrón.
> You mark: an **X** under *preterite*.

	Present	**Preterite**
Modelo	_____	____**X**____
1.	_____	_____
2.	_____	_____
3.	_____	_____
4.	_____	_____
5.	_____	_____
6.	_____	_____
7.	_____	_____
8.	_____	_____

2 **Cambiar** Change each sentence from the present to the preterite. Repeat the correct answer after the speaker. (*8 items*)

> *modelo*
> Compro unas sandalias baratas.
> *Compré unas sandalias baratas.*

3 **Preguntas** Answer each question you hear using the cue in your lab manual. Repeat the correct response after the speaker.

> *modelo*
> You hear: ¿Dónde conseguiste tus botas?
> You see: en la tienda Lacayo
> You say: *Conseguí mis botas en la tienda Lacayo.*

1. $26,00   2. ayer   3. Marta   4. no   5. no   6. no

4 **¿Estás listo?** Listen to this conversation between Matilde and Hernán. Make a list of the tasks Hernán has already done in preparation for his trip and a list of the tasks he still needs to do.

Tareas completadas

_____

_____

_____

_____

Tareas que necesita hacer

_____

_____

_____

_____

6.4 Demonstrative adjectives and pronouns

1 **En el mercado** A group of tourists is shopping at an open-air market. Listen to what they say, and mark an **X** in the column for the demonstrative adjective you hear.

> **modelo**
> *You hear:* Me gusta mucho esa bolsa.
> *You mark:* an **X** under *that*.

	this	that	these	those
Modelo	_____	**X** _____	_____	_____
1.	_____	_____	_____	_____
2.	_____	_____	_____	_____
3.	_____	_____	_____	_____
4.	_____	_____	_____	_____

2 **Cambiar** Form a new sentence using the cue you hear. Repeat the correct answer after the speaker. (*6 items*)

> **modelo**
> Quiero este suéter. (chaqueta)
> *Quiero esta chaqueta.*

3 **Transformar** Form a new sentence using the cue you hear. Repeat the correct answer after the speaker. (*6 items*)

> **modelo**
> Aquel abrigo es muy hermoso. (corbatas)
> *Aquellas corbatas son muy hermosas.*

4 **Preguntas** Answer each question you hear in the negative using a form of the demonstrative pronoun **ése**. Repeat the correct response after the speaker. (*8 items*)

> **modelo**
> ¿Quieres esta blusa?
> *No, no quiero ésa.*

5 **De compras** Listen to this conversation. Then read the statements in your lab manual and decide whether they are **cierto** or **falso**.

	Cierto	Falso
1. Flor quiere ir al almacén Don Guapo.	O	O
2. Enrique trabaja en el almacén Don Guapo.	O	O
3. El centro comercial está lejos de los chicos.	O	O
4. Van al almacén que está al lado del Hotel Plaza.	O	O

vocabulario

You will now hear the vocabulary for **Lección 6** found on page 200 of your textbook. Listen and repeat each Spanish word or phrase after the speaker.

recursos

Lab CDs/MP3s
Lección 7

contextos

Lección 7

1 **Describir** For each drawing, you will hear two statements. Choose the one that corresponds to the drawing.

1. a. _____ b. _____   2. a. _____ b. _____

11:05 p.m.

3. a. _____ b. _____   4. a. _____ b. _____

2 **Preguntas** Clara is going to baby-sit your nephew. Answer her questions about your nephew's daily routine using the cues in your lab manual. Repeat the correct response after the speaker.

> **modelo**
>
> *You hear:* ¿A qué hora va a la escuela?
> *You see:* 8:30 A.M.
> *You say:* Va a la escuela a las ocho y media de la mañana.

1. 7:00 A.M.   4. champú para niños
2. se lava la cara   5. 9:00 P.M.
3. por la noche   6. después de comer

3 **Entrevista** Listen to this interview. Then read the statements in your lab manual and decide whether they are **cierto** or **falso**.

	Cierto	Falso
1. Sergio Santos es jugador de fútbol.	○	○
2. Sergio se levanta a las 5:00 A.M.	○	○
3. Sergio se ducha por la mañana y por la noche.	○	○
4. Sergio se acuesta a las 11:00 P.M.	○	○

pronunciación

The consonants **r** and **rr**

In Spanish, **r** has a strong trilled sound at the beginning of a word. No English words have a trill, but English speakers often produce a trill when they imitate the sound of a motor.

ropa   rutina   rico   **R**amón

In any other position, **r** has a weak sound similar to the English *tt* in *better* or the English *dd* in *ladder*. In contrast to English, the tongue touches the roof of the mouth behind the teeth.

gusta**r**   du**r**ante   p**r**imero   c**r**ema

The letter **rr**, which only appears between vowels, always has a strong trilled sound.

piza**rr**a   co**rr**o   ma**rr**ón   abu**rr**ido

Between vowels, the difference between the strong trilled **rr** and the weak **r** is very important, as a mispronunciation could lead to confusion between two different words.

caro   carro   pero   perro

---

1 **Práctica** Repeat each word after the speaker, to practice the **r** and the **rr**.

1. Perú	5. comprar	9. Arequipa
2. Rosa	6. favor	10. tarde
3. borrador	7. rubio	11. cerrar
4. madre	8. reloj	12. despertador

---

2 **Oraciones** When you hear the number, read the corresponding sentence aloud, focusing on the **r** and **rr** sounds. Then listen to the speaker and repeat the sentence.

1. Ramón Robles Ruiz es programador. Su esposa Rosaura es artista.
2. A Rosaura Robles le encanta regatear en el mercado.
3. Ramón nunca regatea… le aburre regatear.
4. Rosaura siempre compra cosas baratas.
5. Ramón no es rico pero prefiere comprar cosas muy caras.
6. ¡El martes Ramón compró un carro nuevo!

---

3 **Refranes** Repeat each saying after the speaker to practice the **r** and the **rr**.

1. Perro que ladra no muerde.
2. No se ganó Zamora en una hora.

---

4 **Dictado** You will hear seven sentences. Each will be said twice. Listen carefully and write what you hear.

1. _____
2. _____
3. _____
4. _____
5. _____
6. _____
7. _____

recursos
Lab CDs/MP3s
Lección 7

estructura

7.1 Reflexive verbs

1 **Describir** For each drawing, you will hear two statements. Choose the one that corresponds to the drawing.

1. a. _____ b. _____   2. a. _____ b. _____

¡A+!

3. a. _____ b. _____   4. a. _____ b. _____

---

2 **Preguntas** Answer each question you hear in the affirmative. Repeat the correct response after the speaker. (7 *items*)

> **modelo**
> ¿Se levantó temprano Rosa?
> Sí, Rosa se levantó temprano.

---

3 **¡Esto fue el colmo *(the last straw)*!** Listen as Julia describes what happened in her dorm yesterday. Then choose the correct ending for each statement in your lab manual.

1. Julia se ducha en cinco minutos porque...
   a. siempre se levanta tarde.   b. las chicas de su piso comparten un cuarto de baño.
2. Ayer la chica nueva...
   a. se quedó dos horas en el baño.   b. se preocupó por Julia.
3. Cuando salió, la chica nueva...
   a. se enojó mucho.   b. se sintió *(felt)* avergonzada.

7.2 Indefinite and negative words

1 **¿Lógico o ilógico?** You will hear some questions and the responses. Decide if they are **lógico** or **ilógico**.

	Lógico	Ilógico			Lógico	Ilógico
1.	○	○		5.	○	○
2.	○	○		6.	○	○
3.	○	○		7.	○	○
4.	○	○		8.	○	○

2 **¿Pero o sino?** You will hear some sentences with a beep in place of a word. Decide if **pero** or **sino** should complete each sentence and circle it.

> modelo
>
> *You hear:* Ellos no viven en Lima *(beep)* en Arequipa.
> *You circle:* sino because the sentence is Ellos *no viven en Lima sino en Arequipa.*

1.	pero	sino		5.	pero	sino
2.	pero	sino		6.	pero	sino
3.	pero	sino		7.	pero	sino
4.	pero	sino		8.	pero	sino

3 **Transformar** Change each sentence you hear to say the opposite is true. Repeat the correct answer after the speaker. (*6 items*)

> modelo
>
> Nadie se ducha ahora.
> Alguien *se ducha ahora.*

4 **Preguntas** Answer each question you hear in the negative. Repeat the correct response after the speaker. (*6 items*)

> modelo
>
> ¿Qué estás haciendo?
> No estoy haciendo nada.

5 **Entre amigos** Listen to this conversation between Felipe and Mercedes. Then decide whether the statements in your lab manual are **cierto** or **falso**.

		Cierto	Falso
1.	No hay nadie en la residencia.	○	○
2.	Mercedes quiere ir al Centro Estudiantil.	○	○
3.	Felipe tiene un amigo peruano.	○	○
4.	Mercedes no visitó ni Machu Picchu ni Cuzco.	○	○
5.	Felipe nunca visitó el Perú.	○	○

7.3 Preterite of **ser** and **ir**

1 **Escoger** Listen to each sentence and indicate whether the verb is a form of **ser** or **ir**.

1. ser   ir
2. ser   ir
3. ser   ir
4. ser   ir

5. ser   ir
6. ser   ir
7. ser   ir
8. ser   ir

2 **Cambiar** Change each sentence from the present to the preterite. Repeat the correct answer after the speaker. (*8 items*)

> modelo
>
> Ustedes van en avión.
> *Ustedes fueron en avión.*

3 **Preguntas** Answer each question you hear using the cue in your lab manual. Repeat the correct response after the speaker.

> modelo
>
> *You hear:* ¿Quién fue tu profesor de química?
> *You see:* el Sr. Ortega
> *You say: El Sr. Ortega fue mi profesor de química.*

1. al mercado al aire libre
2. muy buenas
3. no

4. fabulosa
5. al parque
6. difícil

4 **¿Qué hicieron (*did they do*) anoche?** Listen to this telephone conversation and answer the questions in your lab manual.

1. ¿Adónde fue Carlos anoche?

_____

2. ¿Cómo fue el partido? ¿Por qué?

_____

3. ¿Adónde fueron Katarina y Esteban anoche?

_____

4. Y Esteban, ¿qué hizo (*did he do*) allí?

_____

7.4 Gustar and verbs like gustar

1 **Escoger** Listen to each question and choose the most logical response.

1. a. Sí, me gusta.   b. Sí, te gusta.
2. a. No, no le interesa.   b. No, no le interesan.
3. a. Sí, les molestan mucho.   b. No, no les molesta mucho.
4. a. No, no nos importa.   b. No, no les importa.
5. a. Sí, le falta.   b. Sí, me falta.
6. a. Sí, les fascina.   b. No, no les fascinan.

2 **Cambiar** Form a new sentence using the cue you hear. Repeat the correct answer after the speaker. (6 items)

modelo
A ellos les interesan las ciencias. (a Ricardo)
A Ricardo le interesan las ciencias.

3 **Preguntas** Answer each question you hear using the cue in your lab manual. Repeat the correct response after the speaker.

modelo
You hear: ¿Qué te encanta hacer?
You see: patinar en línea
You say: Me encanta patinar en línea.

1. la familia y los amigos   4. $2,00   7. no / nada
2. sí   5. el baloncesto y el béisbol   8. sí
3. las computadoras   6. no

4 **Preferencias** Listen to this conversation. Then fill in the chart with Eduardo's preferences and answer the question in your lab manual.

Le gusta	No le gusta

¿Que van a hacer los chicos esta tarde? _____

vocabulario

You will now hear the vocabulary for **Lección 7** found on page 232 of your textbook. Listen and repeat each Spanish word or phrase after the speaker.

recursos

Lab CDs/MP3s
Lección 8

contextos

Lección 8

1 **Identificar** Listen to each question and mark an **X** in the appropriate category.

	carne	pescado	verdura	fruta	bebida
Modelo	_____	_____	_____	**X**	_____
1.	_____	_____	_____	_____	_____
2.	_____	_____	_____	_____	_____
3.	_____	_____	_____	_____	_____
4.	_____	_____	_____	_____	_____
5.	_____	_____	_____	_____	_____
6.	_____	_____	_____	_____	_____
7.	_____	_____	_____	_____	_____
8.	_____	_____	_____	_____	_____

2 **Describir** Listen to each sentence and write the number of the sentence below the drawing of the food or drink mentioned.

a. _____ b. _____ c. _____ d. _____

e. _____ f. _____ g. _____ h. _____

i. _____ j. _____

3 **En el restaurante** You will hear a couple ordering a meal in a restaurant. Write the items they order in the appropriate categories.

	SEÑORA	SEÑOR
Primer plato		
Plato principal		
Verdura		
Bebida		

pronunciación

ll, ñ, c, and z

Most Spanish speakers pronounce the letter **ll** like the *y* in *yes*.

| po**ll**o | **ll**ave | e**ll**a | cebo**ll**a |

The letter **ñ** is pronounced much like the *ny* in *canyon*.

| ma**ñ**ana | se**ñ**or | ba**ñ**o | ni**ñ**a |

Before **a, o,** or **u,** the Spanish **c** is pronounced like the *c* in *car*.

| **c**afé | **c**olombiano | **c**uando | ri**c**o |

Before **e** or **i,** the Spanish **c** is pronounced like the *s* in *sit*. In parts of Spain, **c** before **e** or **i** is pronounced like the *th* in *think*.

| **c**ereales | deli**c**ioso | condu**c**ir | cono**c**er |

The Spanish **z** is pronounced like the *s* in *sit*. In parts of Spain, **z** before a vowel is pronounced like the *th* in *think*.

| **z**eta | **z**anahoria | almuer**z**o | cerve**z**a |

1 Práctica Repeat each word after the speaker to practice pronouncing **ll, ñ, c,** and **z.**

1. mantequilla
2. cuñado
3. aceite
4. manzana
5. español
6. cepillo
7. zapato
8. azúcar
9. quince
10. compañera
11. almorzar
12. calle

2 Oraciones When the speaker pauses, repeat the corresponding sentence or phrase, focusing on **ll, ñ, c,** and **z.**

1. Mi compañero de cuarto se llama Tonio Núñez. Su familia es de la ciudad de Guatemala y de Quetzaltenango.
2. Dice que la comida de su mamá es deliciosa, especialmente su pollo al champiñón y sus tortillas de maíz.
3. Creo que Toño tiene razón porque hoy cené en su casa y quiero volver mañana para cenar allí otra vez.

3 Refranes Repeat each saying after the speaker to practice pronouncing **ll, ñ, c,** and **z.**

1. Las aparencias engañan.
2. Panza llena, corazón contento.

4 Dictado You will hear five sentences. Each will be said twice. Listen carefully and write what you hear.

1. _____
2. _____
3. _____
4. _____
5. _____

recursos

Lab CDs/MP3s
Lección 8

estructura

8.1 Preterite of stem-changing verbs

1 **Identificar** Listen to each sentence and decide whether the verb is in the present or the preterite tense. Mark an **X** in the appropriate column.

> *modelo*
> *You hear:* Pido bistec con papas fritas.
> *You mark:* an **X** under *Present.*

	Present	Preterite
Modelo _____	**X**	_____
1. _____	_____	_____
2. _____	_____	_____
3. _____	_____	_____
4. _____	_____	_____
5. _____	_____	_____
6. _____	_____	_____
7. _____	_____	_____
8. _____	_____	_____

2 **Cambiar** Change each sentence you hear substituting the new subject given. Repeat the correct response after the speaker. (*6 items*)

> *modelo*
> Tú no dormiste bien anoche. (Los niños)
> *Los niños no durmieron bien anoche.*

3 **Preguntas** Answer each questions you hear using the cue in your lab manual. Repeat the correct response after the speaker.

> *modelo*
> *You hear:* ¿Qué pediste?
> *You see:* pavo asado con papas y arvejas
> *You say: Pedí pavo asado con papas y arvejas.*

1. Sí   3. leche   5. No
2. No   4. Sí   6. la semana pasada

4 **Un día largo** Listen as Ernesto describes what he did yesterday. Then read the statements in your lab manual and decide whether they are **cierto** or **falso**.

	Cierto	Falso
1. Ernesto se levantó a las seis y media de la mañana.	○	○
2. Se bañó y se vistió.	○	○
3. Los clientes empezaron a llegar a la una.	○	○
4. Almorzó temprano.	○	○
5. Pidió pollo asado con papas.	○	○
6. Después de almorzar, Ernesto y su primo siguieron trabajando.	○	○

8.2 Double object pronouns

1 **Escoger** The manager of **El Gran Pavo** Restaurant wants to know what items the chef is going to serve to the customers today. Listen to each question and choose the correct response.

1. a. Sí, se las voy a servir. b. No, no se los voy a servir.

2. a. Sí, se la voy a servir. b. No, no se lo voy a servir.

3. a. Sí, se los voy a servir. b. No, no se las voy a servir.

4. a. Sí, se los voy a servir. b. No, no se las voy a servir.

5. a. Sí, se la voy a servir. b. No, no se lo voy a servir.

6. a. Sí, se lo voy a servir. b. No, no se la voy a servir.

2 **Cambiar** Repeat each statement, replacing the direct object noun with a pronoun. (6 *items*)

> modelo
> María te hace ensalada.
> María *te la hace.*

3 **Preguntas** Answer each question using the cue you hear and object pronouns. Repeat the correct response after the speaker. (5 *items*)

> modelo
> ¿Me recomienda usted los mariscos? (Sí)
> Sí, *se los recomiendo.*

4 **Una fiesta** Listen to this conversation between Eva and Marcela. Then read the statements in your lab manual and decide whether they are **cierto** or **falso**.

	Cierto	Falso
1. Le van a hacer una fiesta a Sebastián.	○	○
2. Le van a preparar langosta.	○	○
3. Le van a preparar una ensalada de mariscos.	○	○
4. Van a tener vino tinto, cerveza, agua mineral y té helado.	○	○
5. Clara va a comprar cerveza.	○	○
6. Le compraron un cinturón.	○	○

8.3 Saber and conocer

1 **¿Saber o conocer?** You will hear some sentences with a beep in place of the verb. Decide which form of **saber** or **conocer** should complete each sentence and circle it.

> **modelo**
> You hear: (Beep) cantar.
> You circle: **Sé** because the sentence is **Sé cantar.**

1. Sé	Conozco	3. Sabemos	Conocemos	5. Sé	Conozco
2. Saben	Conocen	4. Sé	Conozco	6. Sabes	Conoces

2 **Cambiar** Listen to the following statements and say that you do the same activities. Repeat the correct answer after the speaker. (*5 items*)

> **modelo**
> Julia sabe nadar.
> Yo también sé nadar.

3 **Preguntas** Answer each question using the cue you hear. Repeat the correct response after the speaker. (*6 items*)

> **modelo**
> ¿Conocen tus padres Antigua? (Sí)
> Sí, mis padres conocen Antigua.

4 **Mi compañera de cuarto** Listen as Jennifer describes her roommate. Then read the statements in your lab manual and decide whether they are **cierto** or **falso**.

	Cierto	Falso
1. Jennifer conoció a Laura en la escuela primaria.	○	○
2. Laura sabe hacer muchas cosas.	○	○
3. Laura sabe hablar alemán.	○	○
4. Laura sabe preparar comida mexicana.	○	○
5. Laura sabe patinar en línea.	○	○
6. Laura conoce a algunos muchachos simpáticos.	○	○

5 **La mejor comida** Listen to this conversation between Jorge and Rosalía. Then choose the correct answers to the questions in your lab manual.

1. ¿Por qué conoce Jorge muchos restaurantes?
   a. Es aficionado a los restaurantes.
   b. Él es camarero.
2. ¿Qué piensa Rosalía de la buena comida?
   a. Piensa que la gente no necesita ir a un restaurante para comer bien.
   b. Piensa que la gente encuentra la mejor comida en un restaurante.
3. ¿Dónde están Jorge y Rosalía?
   a. Están en la universidad.
   b. Están trabajando.
4. ¿Sabe Rosalía dónde está el restaurante?
   a. Sí, lo sabe.
   b. No lo conoce.

8.4 Comparisons and superlatives

1 **Escoger** You will hear a series of descriptions. Choose the statement in your lab manual that expresses the correct comparison.

1. a. Yo tengo más dinero que Rafael.
   b. Yo tengo menos dinero que Rafael.
2. a. Elena es mayor que Juan.
   b. Elena es menor que Juan.
3. a. Enrique come más hamburguesas que José.
   b. Enrique come tantas hamburguesas como José.
4. a. La comida de la Fonda es mejor que la comida del Café Condesa
   b. La comida de la Fonda es peor que la comida del Café Condesa.
5. a. Las langostas cuestan tanto como los camarones.
   b. Los camarones cuestan menos que las langostas.

2 **Comparar** Look at each drawing and answer the question you hear with a comparative statement. Repeat the correct response after the speaker.

1.   Ricardo   Sara

2.   Héctor   Alejandro

3.   Leonor   Melissa

3 **Al contrario** You are babysitting Anita, a small child, who starts boasting about herself and her family. Respond to each statement using a comparative of equality. Then repeat the correct answer after the speaker. (6 *items*)

> *modelo*
> Mi mamá es más bonita que tu mamá.
> Al contrario, mi mamá es tan bonita como tu mamá.

4 **Preguntas** Answer each question you hear using the absolute superlative. Repeat the correct response after the speaker. (5 *items*)

> *modelo*
> La comida de la cafetería es mala, ¿no?
> Sí, es malísima.

vocabulario

You will now hear the vocabulary for **Lección 8** found on page 268 of your textbook. Listen and repeat each Spanish word or phrase after the speaker.

recursos

Lab CDs/MP3s
Lección 9

contextos

Lección 9

1 **¿Lógico o ilógico?** You will hear some statements. Decide if they are **lógico** or **ilógico**.

1. Lógico	Ilógico	5. Lógico	Ilógico
2. Lógico	Ilógico	6. Lógico	Ilógico
3. Lógico	Ilógico	7. Lógico	Ilógico
4. Lógico	Ilógico	8. Lógico	Ilógico

2 **Escoger** For each drawing, you will hear three statements. Choose the one that corresponds to the drawing.

1. a.   b.   c.

2. a.   b.   c.

3. a.   b.   c.

4. a.   b.   c.

3 **Una celebración** Listen as Sra. Jiménez talks about a party she has planned. Then answer the questions in your lab manual.

1. ¿Para quién es la fiesta?

_____

2. ¿Cuándo es la fiesta?

_____

3. ¿Por qué hacen la fiesta?

_____

4. ¿Quiénes van a la fiesta?

_____

5. ¿Qué van a hacer los invitados en la fiesta?

_____

pronunciación

The letters **h**, **j**, and **g**

The Spanish **h** is always silent.

helado	**h**ombre	**h**ola	**h**ermosa

The letter **j** is pronounced much like the English *h* in *his*.

José	**j**ubilarse	de**j**ar	pare**j**a

The letter **g** can be pronounced three different ways. Before **e** or **i**, the letter **g** is pronounced much like the English *h*.

a**g**encia	**g**eneral	**G**il	**G**isela

At the beginning of a phrase or after the letter **n**, the Spanish **g** is pronounced like the English *g* in *girl*.

Gustavo, **g**racias por llamar el domin**g**o.

In any other position, the Spanish **g** has a somewhat softer sound.

Me **g**radué en a**g**osto.

In the combinations **gue** and **gui**, the **g** has a hard sound and the **u** is silent. In the combination **gua**, the **g** has a hard sound and the **u** is pronounced like the English *w*.

Guerra	conse**gui**r	**gua**ntes	a**gua**

1 **Práctica** Repeat each word after the speaker to practice pronouncing **h**, **j**, and **g**.

1. hamburguesa	4. guapa	7. espejo	10. gracias	13. Jorge
2. jugar	5. geografía	8. hago	11. hijo	14. tengo
3. oreja	6. magnífico	9. seguir	12. galleta	15. ahora

2 **Oraciones** When you hear the number, read the corresponding sentence aloud. Then listen to the speaker and repeat the sentence.

1. Hola. Me llamo Gustavo Hinojosa Lugones y vivo en Santiago de Chile.
2. Tengo una familia grande; somos tres hermanos y tres hermanas.
3. Voy a graduarme en mayo.
4. Para celebrar mi graduación mis padres van a regalarme un viaje a Egipto.
5. ¡Qué generosos son!

3 **Refranes** Repeat each saying after the speaker to practice pronouncing **h**, **j**, and **g**.

1. A la larga, lo más dulce amarga.
2. El hábito no hace al monje.

4 **Dictado** Victoria is talking to her friend Mirta on the phone. Listen carefully and during the pauses write what she says. The entire passage will then be repeated so that you can check your work.

_____

_____

_____

estructura

9.1 Irregular preterites

1 **Escoger** Listen to each question and choose the most logical response.

1. a. No, no conduje hoy.   b. No, no condujo hoy.
2. a. Te dije que tengo una cita con   b. Me dijo que tiene una cita con
   Gabriela esta noche.   Gabriela esta noche.
3. a. Estuvimos en la casa de Marta.   b. Estuvieron en la casa de Marta.
4. a. Porque tuvo que estudiar.   b. Porque tiene que estudiar.
5. a. Lo supieron la semana pasada.   b. Lo supimos la semana pasada.
6. a. Los pusimos en la mesa.   b. Los pusiste en la mesa.
7. a. No, sólo tradujimos un poco.   b. No, sólo traduje un poco.
8. a. Sí, le di $20.000.   b. Sí, le dio $20.000.

2 **Cambiar** Change each sentence from the present to the preterite. Repeat the correct answer after the speaker. (*8 items*)

> **modelo**
> Él pone el flan sobre la mesa.
> Él *puso el flan sobre la mesa.*

3 **Preguntas** Answer each question you hear using the cue in your lab manual. Substitute object pronouns for the direct object when possible. Repeat the correct answer after the speaker.

> **modelo**
> *You hear:* ¿Quién condujo el auto?
> *You see:* yo
> *You say:* Yo lo conduje.

1. Gerardo   3. nosotros   5. ¡Felicitaciones!
2. Mateo y Yolanda   4. muy buena   6. mi papá

4 **Completar** Listen to the dialogue and write the missing words in your lab manual.

(1) _____ por un amigo que los Márquez (2) _____ a visi-

tar a su hija. Me (3) _____ que (4) _____ desde

Antofagasta y que se (5) _____ en el Hotel Carrera. Les

(6) _____ una llamada (*call*) anoche pero no (7) _____ el

teléfono. Sólo (8) _____ dejarles un mensaje. Hoy ellos me

(9) _____ y me (10) _____ si mi esposa y yo teníamos

tiempo para almorzar con ellos. Claro que les (11) _____ que sí.

9.2 Verbs that change meaning in the preterite

1 **Identificar** Listen to each sentence and mark and **X** in the column for the subject of the verb.

> **modelo**
> *You hear:* ¿Cuándo lo supiste?
> *You mark:* an **X** under **tú.**

	yo	tú	ella	nosotros	ellos
Modelo	_____	**X**	_____	_____	_____
1. _____	_____	_____	_____	_____	_____
2. _____	_____	_____	_____	_____	_____
3. _____	_____	_____	_____	_____	_____
4. _____	_____	_____	_____	_____	_____
5. _____	_____	_____	_____	_____	_____
6. _____	_____	_____	_____	_____	_____
7. _____	_____	_____	_____	_____	_____
8. _____	_____	_____	_____	_____	_____

2 **Preguntas** Answer each question you hear using the cue in your lab manual. Substitute object pronouns for the direct object when possible. Repeat the correct response after the speaker.

> **modelo**
> *You hear:* ¿Conocieron ellos a Sandra?
> *You see:* sí
> *You say:* Sí, la conocieron.

1. sí   2. en la casa de Ángela   3. el viernes   4. no   5. no   6. anoche

3 **¡Qué lástima! (What a shame!)** Listen as José talks about some news he recently received. Then read the statements and decide whether they are **cierto** or **falso**.

	Cierto	Falso
1. Supieron de la muerte ayer.	○	○
2. Se sonrieron cuando oyeron las noticias (*news*).	○	○
3. Carolina no se pudo comunicar con la familia.	○	○
4. Francisco era (*was*) joven.	○	○
5. Mañana piensan llamar a la familia de Francisco.	○	○

4 **Relaciones amorosas** Listen as Susana describes what happened between her and Pedro. Then answer the questions in your lab manual.

1. ¿Por qué no pudo salir Susana con Pedro? _____

2. ¿Qué supo por su amiga? _____

3. ¿Cómo se puso ella cuando Pedro llamó? _____

4. ¿Qué le dijo Susana a Pedro? _____

9.3 ¿Qué? and ¿cuál?

1 **¿Lógico o ilógico?** You will hear some questions and the responses. Decide if they are **lógico** or **ilógico**.

1. Lógico   Ilógico   5. Lógico   Ilógico
2. Lógico   Ilógico   6. Lógico   Ilógico
3. Lógico   Ilógico   7. Lógico   Ilógico
4. Lógico   Ilógico   8. Lógico   Ilógico

2 **Preguntas** You will hear a series of responses to questions. Using **¿qué?** or **¿cuál?**, form the question that prompted each response. Repeat the correct answer after the speaker. (*8 items*)

> **modelo**
> Santiago de Chile es la capital de Chile.
> *¿Cuál es la capital de Chile?*

3 **De compras** Look at Marcela's shopping list for Christmas and answer each question you hear. Repeat the correct response after the speaker. (*6 items*)

Raúl	2 camisas, talla 17
Cristina	blusa, color azul
Pepe	bluejeans y tres pares de calcetines blancos
Abuelo	cinturón
Abuela	suéter blanco

4 **Escoger** Listen to this radio commercial and choose the most logical response to each question.

1. ¿Qué hace Fiestas Mar?
   a. Organiza fiestas.   b. Es una tienda que vende cosas para fiestas.   c. Es un club en el mar.
2. ¿Para qué tipo de fiesta no usaría Fiestas Mar?
   a. Para una boda.   b. Para una fiesta de sorpresa.   c. Para una cena con los suegros.
3. ¿Cuál de estos servicios no ofrece Fiestas Mar?
   a. Poner las decoraciones.   b. Proveer (*Provide*) el lugar.   c. Proveer los regalos.
4. ¿Qué tiene que hacer el cliente si usa Fiestas Mar?
   a. Tiene que preocuparse por la lista de invitados.   b. Tiene que preocuparse por la música.
   c. Tiene que preparar la comida.
5. Si uno quiere contactar Fiestas Mar, ¿qué debe hacer?
   a. Debe escribirles un mensaje electrónico.   b. Debe llamarlos.   c. Debe ir a Casa Mar.

9.4 Pronouns after prepositions

1   **Cambiar**   Listen to each statement and say that the feeling is not mutual. Use a pronoun after the preposition in your response. Then repeat the correct answer after the speaker. (*6 items*)

> *modelo*
> Carlos quiere desayunar con nosotros.
> *Pero nosotros no queremos desayunar con él.*

2   **Preguntas**   Answer each question you hear using the appropriate pronoun after the preposition and the cue in your lab manual. Repeat the correct response after the speaker.

> *modelo*
> *You hear:* ¿Almuerzas con Alberto hoy?
> *You see:* No
> *You say:* No, no almuerzo con él hoy.

1. Sí
2. Luis
3. Sí
4. Sí
5. No
6. Francisco

3   **Preparativos (*Preparations*)**   Listen to this conversation between David and Andrés. Then answer the questions in your lab manual.

1. ¿Qué necesitan comprar para la fiesta?

   _____

2. ¿Con quién quiere Alfredo ir a la fiesta?

   _____

3. ¿Por qué ella no quiere ir con él?

   _____

4. ¿Con quién va Sara?

   _____

5. ¿Para quién quieren comprar algo especial?

   _____

vocabulario

You will now hear the vocabulary for **Lección 9** found on page 296 of your textbook. Listen and repeat each Spanish word or phrase after the speaker.

contextos

Lección 10

1 **Identificar** You will hear a series of words. Write each one in the appropriate category.

> **modelo**
> *You hear:* el hospital
> *You write:* el **hospital** under **Lugares.**

Lugares	Medicinas	Condiciones y síntomas médicos
el hospital		

2 **Describir** For each drawing, you will hear two statements. Choose the one that corresponds to the drawing.

1. a. _____ b. _____

2. a. _____ b. _____

3. a. _____ b. _____

4. a. _____ b. _____

pronunciación

c (before a consonant) and q

In Lesson 8, you learned that, in Spanish, the letter **c** before the vowels **a, o,** and **u** is pronounced like the *c* in the English word *car*. When the letter **c** appears before any consonant except **h,** it is also pronounced like the *c* in *car*.

clínica	bici**cl**eta	**cr**ema	do**ct**ora	o**ct**ubre

In Spanish, the letter **q** is always followed by an **u**, which is silent. The combination **qu** is pronounced like the *k* sound in the English word *kitten*. Remember that the sounds **kwa, kwe, kwi, kwo,** and **koo** are always spelled with the combination **cu** in Spanish, never with **qu**.

querer	par**qu**e	**qu**eso	**qu**ímica	mante**qu**illa

---

1 **Práctica** Repeat each word after the speaker, focusing on the **c** and **q** sounds.

1. quince	5. conductor	9. aquí
2. querer	6. escribir	10. ciclismo
3. pequeño	7. contacto	11. electrónico
4. equipo	8. increíble	12. quitarse

---

2 **Oraciones** When you hear the number, read the corresponding sentence aloud. Then listen to the speaker and repeat the sentence.

1. El Dr. Cruz quiso sacarle la muela.
2. Clara siempre se maquilla antes de salir de casa.
3. ¿Quién perdió su equipaje?
4. Pienso comprar aquella camisa porque me queda bien.
5. La chaqueta cuesta quinientos cuarenta dólares, ¿no?
6. Esa cliente quiere pagar con tarjeta de crédito.

---

3 **Refranes** Repeat each saying after the speaker to practice the **c** and the **q** sounds.

1. Ver es creer. [1]
2. Quien mal anda, mal acaba. [2]

---

4 **Dictado** You will hear five sentences. Each will be said twice. Listen carefully and write what you hear.

1. _____

2. _____

3. _____

4. _____

5. _____

_____

Seeing is believing. [1]
He who lives badly, ends badly. [2]

---

recursos

Lab CDs/MP3s
Lección 10

estructura

10.1 The imperfect tense

1 **Identificar** Listen to each sentence and circle the verb tense you hear.

1. a. present   b. preterite   c. imperfect   6. a. present   b. preterite   c. imperfect
2. a. present   b. preterite   c. imperfect   7. a. present   b. preterite   c. imperfect
3. a. present   b. preterite   c. imperfect   8. a. present   b. preterite   c. imperfect
4. a. present   b. preterite   c. imperfect   9. a. present   b. preterite   c. imperfect
5. a. present   b. preterite   c. imperfect   10. a. present   b. preterite   c. imperfect

2 **Cambiar** Form a new sentence using the cue you hear. Repeat the correct answer after the speaker. (6 *items*)

> modelo
>
> Iban a casa. (Eva)
> Eva iba a casa.

3 **Preguntas** A reporter is writing an article about funny things people used to do when they were children. Answer her questions, using the cues in your lab manual. Then repeat the correct response after the speaker.

> modelo
>
> You hear: ¿Qué hacía Miguel de niño?
> You see: ponerse pajitas (*straws*) en la nariz
> You say: Miguel se ponía pajitas en la nariz.

1. quitarse los zapatos en el restaurante   4. jugar con un amigo invisible
2. vestirnos con la ropa de mamá   5. usar las botas de su papá
3. sólo querer comer dulces   6. comer con las manos

4 **Completar** Listen to this description of Ángela's medical problem and write the missing words in your lab manual.

(1) _____ Ángela porque (2) _____ día y noche.

(3) _____ que (4) _____ un resfriado, pero se

(5) _____ bastante saludable. Se (6) _____ de la biblioteca después

de poco tiempo porque les (7) _____ a los otros estudiantes. Sus amigas, Laura y

Petra, siempre le (8) _____ que (9) _____ alguna alergia. Por fin,

decidió hacerse un examen médico. La doctora le dijo que ella (10) _____

alérgica y que (11) _____ muchas medicinas para las alergias. Finalmente, le

recetó unas pastillas. Al día siguiente (*following*), Ángela se (12) _____ mejor

porque (13) _____ cuál era el problema y ella dejó de estornudar después de

tomar las pastillas.

10.2 The preterite and the imperfect

1 Identificar Listen to each statement and identify the verbs in the preterite and the imperfect. Write them in the appropriate column.

> **modelo**
>
> *You hear:* Cuando llegó la ambulancia, el esposo estaba mareado.
> *You write:* **llegó** under *preterite*, and **estaba** under *imperfect*.

	preterite	imperfect
Modelo	llegó	estaba
1.		
2.		
3.		
4.		
5.		
6.		
7.		
8.		

2 Responder Answer the questions using the cues in your lab manual. Substitute direct object pronouns for the direct object nouns when appropriate. Repeat the correct response after the speaker.

> **modelo**
>
> *You hear:* ¿Por qué no llamaste al médico la semana pasada?
> *You see:* perder su número de teléfono
> *You say:* Porque perdí su número de teléfono.

1. en la mesa de la cocina
2. tener ocho años
3. lastimar el tobillo
4. no, poner en la mochila
5. tomar las pastillas
6. No. Pero tener una grave infección de garganta.
7. toda la mañana
8. necesitar una radiografía de la boca

3 ¡Qué nervios! Listen as Sandra tells a friend about her day. Then read the statments in your lab manual and decide whether they are **cierto** or **falso**.

	Cierto	Falso
1. Sandra tenía mucha experiencia poniendo inyecciones.	○	○
2. La enfermera tenía un terrible dolor de cabeza.	○	○
3. La enfermera le dio una pastilla a Sandra.	○	○
4. El paciente trabajaba en el hospital con Sandra.	○	○
5. El paciente estaba muy nervioso.	○	○
6. Sandra le puso la inyección mientras él hablaba.	○	○

10.3 Constructions with se

1 **Escoger** Listen to each question and choose the most logical response.

1. a. Ay, se te quedó en casa.
   b. Ay, se me quedó en casa.
2. a. No, se le olvidó llamarlo.
   b. No, se me olvidó llamarlo.
3. a. Se le rompieron jugando al fútbol.
   b. Se les rompieron jugando al fútbol.

4. a. Ay, se les olvidaron.
   b. Ay, se nos olvidaron.
5. a. No, se me perdió.
   b. No se le perdió.
6. a. Se nos rompió.
   b. Se le rompieron.

2 **Preguntas** Answer each question you hear using the cue in your lab manual and the impersonal **se**. Repeat the correct response after the speaker.

> **modelo**
> You hear: ¿Qué lengua se habla en Costa Rica?
> You see: español
> You say: Se habla español.

1. a las seis
2. gripe
3. en la farmacia

4. en la caja
5. en la Oficina de Turismo
6. tomar el autobús #3

3 **Letreros (Signs)** Some or all of the type is missing on the signs in your lab manual. Listen to the speaker and write the appropriate text below each sign. The text for each sign will be repeated.

_____

_____

_____

_____

_____

_____

_____

_____

_____

_____

10.4 Adverbs

1 **Completar** Listen to each statement and circle the word or phrase that best completes it.

1. a. casi   b. mal   c. ayer
2. a. con frecuencia   b. además   c. ayer
3. a. poco   b. tarde   c. bien
4. a. a menudo   b. muy   c. menos
5. a. así   b. apenas   c. tranquilamente
6. a. bastante   b. a tiempo   c. normalmente

2 **Cambiar** Form a new sentence by changing the adjective in your lab manual to an adverb. Repeat the correct answer after the speaker.

> **modelo**
> *You hear:* Juan dibuja.
> *You see:* fabuloso
> *You say:* Juan dibuja fabulosamente.

1. regular   4. constante
2. rápido   5. general
3. feliz   6. fácil

3 **Preguntas** Answer each question you hear in the negative, using the cue in your lab manual. Repeat the correct response after the speaker.

> **modelo**
> *You hear:* ¿Salió bien la operación?
> *You see:* mal
> *You say:* No, la operación salió mal.

1. lentamente   4. nunca
2. tarde   5. tristemente
3. muy   6. poco

4 **Situaciones** You will hear four brief conversations. Choose the phrase that best completes each sentence in your lab manual.

1. Mónica…
   a. llegó tarde al aeropuerto.
   b. casi perdió el avión a San José.
   c. decidió no ir a San José.

2. Pilar…
   a. se preocupa por la salud de Tomás.
   b. habla con su médico.
   c. habla con Tomás sobre un problema médico.

3. La Sra. Blanco…
   a. se rompió la pierna hoy.
   b. quiere saber si puede correr mañana.
   c. se lastimó el tobillo hoy.

4. María está enojada porque Vicente…
   a. no va a recoger (*to pick up*) su medicina.
   b. no recogió su medicina ayer.
   c. no debe tomar antibióticos.

vocabulario

You will now hear the vocabulary for **Lección 10** found on page 328 of your textbook. Listen and repeat each Spanish word or phrase after the speaker.

contextos

Lección 11

---

1 **Asociaciones** Circle the word or words that are not logically associated with each word you hear.

1. la impresora	la velocidad	el *fax*
2. guardar	imprimir	funcionar
3. la carretera	el motor	el sitio Web
4. el tanque	el ratón	el aceite
5. conducir	el cibercafé	el *walkman*
6. el archivo	la televisión	la llanta

---

2 **¿Lógico o ilógico?** You will hear some statements. Decide if they are **lógico** or **ilógico**.

	Lógico	Ilógico			Lógico	Ilógico
1.	○	○		4.	○	○
2.	○	○		5.	○	○
3.	○	○		6.	○	○

---

3 **Identificar** For each drawing in your lab manual, you will hear two statements. Choose the statement that best corresponds to the drawing.

1. a. _____ b. _____   2. a. _____ b. _____

3. a. _____ b. _____   4. a. _____ b. _____

---

recursos

Lab CDs/MP3s
Lección 11

pronunciación

c (before e or i), s, and z

In Latin America, **c** before **e** or **i** sounds much like the *s* in *sit*.

medi**c**ina   **c**elular   cono**c**er   pa**c**iente

In parts of Spain, **c** before **e** or **i** is pronounced like the *th* in *think*.

condu**c**ir   poli**c**ía   **c**ederrón   velo**c**idad

The letter **s** is pronounced like the *s* in *sit*.

subir   be**s**ar   **s**onar   impre**s**ora

In Latin America, the Spanish **z** is pronounced like the s in *sit*.

cabe**z**a   nari**z**   abra**z**ar   embara**z**ada

The **z** is pronounced like the *th* in *think* in parts of Spain.

zapatos   **z**ona   pla**z**a   bra**z**o

---

1 **Práctica** Repeat each word after the speaker to practice pronouncing **s**, **z**, and **c** before **i** and **e**.

1. funcionar   4. sitio   7. zanahoria   10. perezoso
2. policía   5. disco   8. marzo   11. quizás
3. receta   6. zapatos   9. comenzar   12. operación

2 **Oraciones** When you hear each number, read the corresponding sentence aloud. Then listen to the speaker and repeat the sentence.

1. Vivió en Buenos Aires en su niñez pero siempre quería pasar su vejez en Santiago.
2. Cecilia y Zulaima fueron al centro a cenar al restaurante Las Delicias.
3. Sonó el despertador a las seis y diez pero estaba cansado y no quiso oírlo.
4. Zacarías jugaba al baloncesto todas las tardes después de cenar.

3 **Refranes** Repeat each saying after the speaker to practice pronouncing **s**, **z**, and **c** before **i** and **e**.

1. Zapatero, a tus zapatos. [1]
2. Primero es la obligación que la devoción. [2]

4 **Dictado** You will hear a friend describing Azucena's weekend experiences. Listen carefully and write what you hear during the pauses. The entire passage will be repeated so that you can check your work.

_____

_____

_____

_____

_____

_____

_____

Mind your P's and Q's. (lit. Shoemaker, to your shoes.) [1]
Business before pleasure. [2]

estructura

11.1 Familiar commands

1 **Identificar** You will hear some sentences. If the verb is a **tú** command, circle **Sí** in your lab manual. If the verb is not a **tú** command, circle **No**.

> **modelo**
> *You hear:* Ayúdanos a encontrar el control remoto.
> *You circle:* **Sí** because **Ayúdanos** is a **tú** *command.*

1. Sí   No
2. Sí   No
3. Sí   No
4. Sí   No
5. Sí   No
6. Sí   No
7. Sí   No
8. Sí   No
9. Sí   No
10. Sí   No

2 **Cambiar** Change each command you hear to the negative. Repeat the correct answer after the speaker. *(8 items)*

> **modelo**
> Cómprame un reproductor de DVD.
> *No me compres un reproductor de DVD.*

3 **Preguntas** Answer each question you hear using an affirmative **tú** command. Repeat the correct response after the speaker. *(7 items)*

> **modelo**
> ¿Estaciono aquí?
> *Sí, estaciona aquí.*

4 **Consejos prácticos** You will hear a conversation among three friends. Using **tú** commands and the ideas presented, write six pieces of advice that Mario can follow to save some money.

1. _____
2. _____
3. _____
4. _____
5. _____
6. _____

11.2 Por and para

1 **Escoger** You will hear some sentences with a beep in place of a preposition. Decide if **por** or **para** should complete each sentence.

> **modelo**
>
> *You hear:* El teclado es (*beep*) la computadora de Nuria.
> *You mark:* an **X** under **para**.

	por	para
Modelo		X
1.		
2.		
3.		
4.		
5.		
6.		
7.		
8.		

2 **La aventura** Complete each phrase about Jaime with **por** or **para** and the cue in your lab manual. Repeat each correct response after the speaker.

> **modelo**
>
> *You hear:* Jaime estudió
> *You see:* médico
> *You say:* **Jaime estudió para médico.**

1. unos meses
2. hacer sus planes
3. mil dólares
4. hacer turismo
5. la ciudad
6. su mamá
7. pesos
8. las montañas

3 **Los planes** Listen to the telephone conversation between Antonio and Sonia and then select the best response for the questions in your lab manual.

1. ¿Por dónde quiere ir Sonia para ir a Bariloche?
   a. Quiere ir por Santiago de Chile.
   b. Va a ir por avión.
2. ¿Para qué va Sonia a Bariloche?
   a. Va para esquiar.
   b. Va para comprar esquíes.
3. ¿Por qué tiene que ir de compras Sonia?
   a. Para comprar una bolsa.
   b. Necesita un abrigo por el frío.
4. ¿Por qué quiere ir Antonio con ella hoy?
   a. Quiere ir para estar con ella.
   b. Quiere ir para comprar un regalo.

11.3 Reciprocal reflexives

1 **Escoger** Listen to each question and, in your lab manual, choose the most logical response.

1. a. Hace cuatro años que nos conocimos.
   b. Se vieron todos los fines de semana.
2. a. Nos besamos antes de salir a trabajar.
   b. Sandra me dijo que no se besaron.
3. a. Nos llevamos mal sólo el último año.
   b. Se llevaron mal siempre.
4. a. Sí, nos saludaban con un abrazo y un beso.
   b. Nos saludaron desde lejos.
5. a. Casi nunca me miraban.
   b. Creo que se miraban con mucho amor.
6. a. Sólo nos ayudamos para el examen.
   b. Se ayudan a menudo.
7. a. Creo que se hablan todas las noches.
   b. Le hablan mucho porque tienen celulares.
8. a. Cuando se casaron se querían mucho.
   b. Cada día nos queremos más.

2 **Responder** Answer each question in the affirmative. Repeat the correct answer after the speaker. (6 *items*)

> modelo
>
> ¿Se abrazaron tú y Carolina en la primera cita?
> Sí, nos abrazamos en la primera cita.

3 **Los amigos** Listen to a description of a friendship and then, in your lab manual, choose the phrase that best completes each sentence.

1. Desde los once años, los chicos _____ con frecuencia.
   a. se veían   b. se ayudaban   c. se besaban
2. Samuel y Andrea _____ por la amistad (*friendship*) de sus madres.
   a. se escribían   b. se entendían   c. se conocieron
3. Las madres de Andrea y Samuel . . .
   a. se ayudaban.   b. se conocían bien.   c. se odiaban.
4. Andrea y Samuel no _____ por un tiempo por un problema.
   a. se conocieron   b. se hablaron   c. se ayudaron
5. Después de un tiempo, . . .
   a. se besaron.   b. se pidieron perdón.   c. se odiaron.
6. La separación sirvió para enseñarles que . . .
   a. se querían.   b. se hablaban mucho.   c. se conocían bien.
7. No es cierto. Andrea y Samuel no . . .
   a. se casaron.   b. se entendían bien.   c. se querían.
8. Los dos amigos _____ por un tiempo.
   a. se besaban   b. se comprometieron   c. se llevaron mal

11.4 Stressed possessive adjectives and pronouns

1   **Identificar**   Listen to each statement and mark an **X** in the column identifying the possessive pronoun you hear.

> **modelo**
>
> *You hear:* Ya arreglaron todos los coches pero el tuyo no.
> *You write:* an **X** under *yours.*

	mine	*yours*	*his/hers*	*ours*	*theirs*
Modelo	_____	**X**	_____	_____	_____
1.	_____	_____	_____	_____	_____
2.	_____	_____	_____	_____	_____
3.	_____	_____	_____	_____	_____
4.	_____	_____	_____	_____	_____
5.	_____	_____	_____	_____	_____
6.	_____	_____	_____	_____	_____
7.	_____	_____	_____	_____	_____
8.	_____	_____	_____	_____	_____

2   **Transformar**   Restate each sentence you hear, using the cues in your lab manual. Repeat the correct answer after the speaker.

> **modelo**
>
> *You hear:* ¿De qué año es el carro suyo?
> *You see:* mine
> *You say:* ¿De qué año es el carro mío?

1. *his*   2. *ours*   3. *yours (fam.)*
4. *theirs*   5. *mine*   6. *hers*

3   **¿Cierto o falso?**   You will hear two brief conversations. Listen carefully and then indicate whether the statements in your lab manual are **cierto** or **falso**.

Conversación 1   **Cierto**   **Falso**

1. Los de la primera conversación comparten sus cosas mejor que los de la segunda.   ○   ○

2. Está claro que los de la primera conversación van a ir a la universidad.   ○   ○

3. Los de la primera conversación van a vivir juntos.   ○   ○

Conversación 2

4. Las personas que hablan o se mencionan en la segunda conversación no saben compartir sus cosas.   ○   ○

5. En la segunda conversación, Adela y su prima hacen planes para sus estudios.   ○   ○

6. En la segunda conversación, Julián necesita la calculadora para sus estudios.   ○   ○

vocabulario

You will now hear the vocabulary for **Lección 11** found on page 360 of your textbook. Listen and repeat each Spanish word or phrase after the speaker.

contextos

Lección 12

1   **Describir**   Listen to each sentence and write the number of the sentence below the drawing of the household item mentioned.

a. _____   b. _____   c. _____

d. _____   e. _____   f. _____

g. _____   h. _____

2   **Identificar**   You will hear a series of words. Write the word that does not belong in each series.

1. _____   4. _____   7. _____

2. _____   5. _____   8. _____

3. _____   6. _____

3   **Quehaceres domésticos**   Your children are complaining about the state of things in your house. Respond to their complaints by telling them what household chores they should do to correct the situation. Repeat the correct response after the speaker. *(6 items)*

> **modelo**
>
> La ropa está arrugada (*wrinkled*).
> *Debes* planchar la ropa.

4   **En la oficina de la agente inmobiliaria**   Listen to this conversation between Mr. Fuentes and a real estate agent. Then read the statements in your lab manual and decide whether they are **cierto** or **falso**.

	Cierto	Falso
1. El Sr. Fuentes quiere alquilar una casa.	○	○
2. El Sr. Fuentes quiere vivir en las afueras.	○	○
3. Él no quiere pagar más de 900 balboas al mes.	○	○
4. Él vive solo (*alone*).	○	○
5. La casa de apartamentos tiene ascensor.	○	○
6. El apartamento tiene lavadora.	○	○

pronunciación

The letter x

In Spanish, the letter **x** has several sounds. When the letter **x** appears between two vowels, it is usually pronounced like the *ks* sound in *eccentric* or the *gs* sound in *egg salad*.

con**ex**ión   **exa**men   **saxo**fón

If the letter x is followed by a consonant, it is pronounced like *s* or *ks*.

e**xp**licar   se**xt**o   e**xc**ursión

In Old Spanish, the letter **x** had the same sound as the Spanish **j**. Some proper names and some words from native languages like Náhuatl and Maya have retained this pronunciation.

Don Qui**x**ote   Oa**x**aca   Te**x**as

---

1 **Práctica** Repeat each word after the speaker, focusing on the **x** sound.

1. éxito
2. reflexivo
3. exterior
4. excelente
5. expedición
6. mexicano
7. expresión
8. examinar
9. excepto
10. exagerar
11. contexto
12. Maximiliano

---

2 **Oraciones** When you hear the number, read the corresponding sentence aloud. Then listen to the speaker and repeat the sentence.

1. Xavier Ximénez va de excursión a Ixtapa.
2. Xavier es una persona excéntrica y se viste de trajes extravagantes.
3. Él es un experto en lenguas extranjeras.
4. Hoy va a una exposición de comidas exóticas.
5. Prueba algunos platos exquisitos y extraordinarios.

---

3 **Refranes** Repeat each saying after the speaker to practice the **x** sound.

1. Ir por extremos no es de discretos.[1]
2. El que de la ira se deja vencer, se expone a perder.[2]

---

4 **Dictado** You will hear five sentences. Each will be said twice. Listen carefully and write what you hear.

1. _____

2. _____

3. _____

4. _____

5. _____

Prudent people don't go to extremes. [1]

He who allows anger to overcome him, risks losing. [2]

recursos

Lab CDs/MP3s
Lección 12

estructura

12.1 Relative pronouns

1 **Escoger** You will hear some sentences with a beep in place of the relative pronoun. Decide whether **que**, **quien**, or **lo que** should complete each sentence and circle it.

> **modelo**
>
> *You hear:* (*Beep*) me gusta de la casa es el jardín.
>
> *You circle:* **Lo que** *because the sentence is* **Lo que me gusta de la casa es el jardín**.

1. que   quien   lo que   6. que   quien   lo que
2. que   quien   lo que   7. Que   Quien   Lo que
3. que   quien   lo que   8. que   quien   lo que
4. que   quien   lo que   9. que   quien   lo que
5. que   quien   lo que   10. que   quien   lo que

2 **Completar** You will hear some incomplete sentences. Choose the correct ending for each sentence.

1. a. con que trabaja tu amiga.
   b. que se mudó a Portobelo.
2. a. que vende muebles baratos.
   b. que trabajábamos.
3. a. a quienes escribí son mis primas.
   b. de quien te escribí.
4. a. con que barres el suelo.
   b. que queremos vender.
5. a. lo que deben.
   b. que deben.
6. a. que te hablo es ama de casa.
   b. en quien pienso es ama de casa.

3 **Preguntas** Answer each question you hear using a relative pronoun and the cues in your lab manual. Repeat the correct response after the speaker.

> **modelo**
>
> *You hear:* ¿Quiénes son los chicos rubios?
> *You see:* mis primos / viven en Colón
> *You say:* **Son mis primos que viven en Colón.**

1. chica / conocí en el café
2. el cliente / llamó ayer
3. chico / se casa Patricia
4. agente / nos ayudó
5. vecinos / viven en la casa azul
6. chica / trabajo

4 **Un robo (*break-in*)** There has been a theft at the Rivera's house. The detective they have hired has gathered all the family members in the living room to reveal the culprit. Listen to his conclusions. Then complete the list of clues (**pistas**) in your lab manual and answer the question.

Pistas

1. El reloj que _____
2. La taza que _____
3. La almohada que _____

Pregunta

¿Quién se llevó las cucharas de la abuela y por qué se las llevó? _____

12.2 Formal commands

1 **Identificar** You will hear some sentences. If the verb is a formal command, circle **Sí**. If the verb is not a command, circle **No**.

> **modelo**
>
> *You hear:* Saque la basura.
> *You circle:* **Sí** *because* **Saque** *is a formal command.*

1. Sí   No
2. Sí   No
3. Sí   No
4. Sí   No
5. Sí   No

6. Sí   No
7. Sí   No
8. Sí   No
9. Sí   No
10. Sí   No

2 **Cambiar** A physician is giving a patient advice. Change each sentence you hear from an indirect command to a formal command. Repeat the correct answer after the speaker. *(6 items)*

> **modelo**
>
> Usted tiene que dormir ocho horas cada noche.
> *Duerma ocho horas cada noche.*

3 **Preguntas** Answer each question you hear in the affirmative using a formal command and a direct object pronoun. Repeat the correct response after the speaker. *(8 items)*

> **modelo**
>
> ¿Cerramos las ventanas?
> *Sí, ciérrenlas.*

4 **Más preguntas** Answer each question you hear using a formal command and the cue in your lab manual. Repeat the correct response after the speaker.

> **modelo**
>
> *You hear:* ¿Debo llamar al Sr. Rodríguez?
> *You see:* no / ahora
> *You say:* No, no lo llame ahora.

1. no
2. a las cinco
3. sí / aquí

4. no
5. el primer día del mes
6. que estamos ocupados

5 **Direcciones** Julia is going to explain how to get to her home. Listen to her instructions, then number the instructions in your lab manual in the correct order. Two items will not be used.

_____ a. entrar al edificio que está al lado del Banco Popular

_____ b. tomar el ascensor al cuarto piso

_____ c. buscar las llaves debajo de la alfombra

_____ d. ir detrás del edificio

_____ e. bajarse del metro en la estación Santa Rosa

_____ f. subir las escaleras al tercer piso

_____ g. caminar hasta el final del pasillo

12.3 The present subjunctive

1   **Escoger**   You will hear some sentences with a beep in place of a verb. Decide which verb should complete each sentence and circle it.

> *modelo*
>
> *You hear:* Es urgente que (*beep*) al médico.
> *You see:* vas   vayas
> *You circle:* **vayas** *because the sentence is* **Es urgente que vayas al médico.**

1. tomamos   tomemos   5. se acuestan   se acuesten
2. conduzcan   conducen   6. sabes   sepas
3. aprenda   aprende   7. almorcemos   almorzamos
4. arreglas   arregles   8. se mude   se muda

2   **Cambiar**   You are a Spanish instructor, and it's the first day of class. Tell your students what it is important for them to do using the cues you hear. *(8 items)*

> *modelo*
>
> hablar español en la clase
> **Es importante que ustedes hablen español en la clase.**

3   **Transformar**   Change each sentence you hear to the subjunctive mood using the expression in your lab manual. Repeat the correct answer after the speaker.

> *modelo*
>
> *You hear:* Pones tu ropa en el armario.
> *You see:* Es necesario
> *You say:* **Es necesario que pongas tu ropa en el armario.**

1. Es mejor   4. Es importante
2. Es urgente   5. Es bueno
3. Es malo   6. Es necesario

4   **¿Qué pasa aquí?**   Listen to this conversation. Then choose the phrase that best completes each sentence in your lab manual.

1. Esta conversación es entre…

    a. un empleado y una clienta.

    b. un hijo y su madre.

    c. un camarero y la dueña de un restaurante.

2. Es necesario que Mario…

    a. llegue temprano.

    b. se lave las manos.

    c. use la lavadora.

3. Es urgente que Mario…

    a. ponga las mesas.

    b. quite las mesas.

    c. sea listo.

12.4 Subjunctive with verbs of will and influence

1 **Identificar** Listen to each sentence. If you hear a verb in the subjunctive, mark **Sí**. If you don't hear the subjunctive, mark **No**.

1. Sí No
2. Sí No
3. Sí No
4. Sí No
5. Sí No
6. Sí No

2 **Transformar** Some people are discussing what they or their friends want to do. Say that you don't want them to do those things. Repeat the correct response after the speaker. *(6 items)*

> modelo
> Esteban quiere invitar a tu hermana a una fiesta.
> **No quiero que Esteban invite a mi hermana a una fiesta.**

3 **Situaciones** Listen to each situation and make a recommendation using the cues in your lab manual. Repeat the correct response after the speaker.

> modelo
> *You hear:* Sacamos una "F" en el examen de química.
> *You see:* estudiar más
> *You say:* **Les recomiendo que estudien más.**

1. ponerte un suéter
2. quedarse en la cama
3. regalarles una tostadora
4. no hacerlo
5. comprarlas en la Casa Bonita
6. ir a La Cascada

4 **¿Qué hacemos?** Listen to this conversation and answer the questions in your lab manual.

1. ¿Qué quiere el Sr. Barriga que hagan los chicos?

_____

2. ¿Qué le pide el chico?

_____

3. ¿Qué les sugiere el señor a los chicos?

_____

4. ¿Qué tienen que hacer los chicos si no consiguen el dinero?

_____

5. Al final, ¿en qué insiste el Sr. Barriga?

_____

vocabulario

You will now hear the vocabulary for **Lección 12** found on page 394 of your textbook. Listen and repeat each Spanish word or phrase after the speaker.

contextos

Lección 13

---

1 **¿Lógico o ilógico?** You will hear some questions and the responses. Decide if they are **lógico** or **ilógico**.

1. Lógico   Ilógico   4. Lógico   Ilógico
2. Lógico   Ilógico   5. Lógico   Ilógico
3. Lógico   Ilógico   6. Lógico   Ilógico

---

2 **Eslóganes** You will hear some slogans created by environmentalists. Write the number of each slogan next to the ecological problem it addresses.

_____ a. la contaminación del aire   _____ d. la contaminación del agua

_____ b. la deforestación   _____ e. la lluvia ácida

_____ c. la extinción de animales   _____ f. la basura en las calles

---

3 **Preguntas** Look at the drawings and answer each question you hear. Repeat the correct response after the speaker.

1.

2.

3.

4.

---

4 **Completar** Listen to this radio advertisement and write the missing words in your lab manual.

Para los que gustan del (1) _____, la agencia Eco-Guías los invita a viajar a la

(2) _____ amazónica. Estar en el Amazonas es convivir (*to coexist*) con la

(3) _____. Venga y (4) _____ los misterios del

(5) _____. Admire de cerca las diferentes (6) _____ y

(7) _____ mientras navega por un (8) _____ que parece

mar. Duerma bajo un (9) _____ lleno de (10) _____.

Piérdase en un (11) _____ de encanto (*enchantment*).

---

recursos

Lab CDs/MP3s
Lección 13

pronunciación

l, ll, and y

In Spanish, the letter **l** is pronounced much like the *l* sound in the English word *lemon*.

    cie**l**o   **l**ago   **l**ata   **l**una

In Lesson 8, you learned that most Spanish speakers pronounce the letter **ll** like the *y* in the English word *yes*. The letter **y** is often pronounced in the same manner.

    estre**ll**a   va**ll**e   ma**y**o   pla**y**a

When the letter **y** occurs at the end of a syllable or by itself, it is pronounced like the Spanish letter **i**.

    le**y**   mu**y**   vo**y**   **y**

1   **Práctica** Repeat each word after the speaker focusing on the **l, ll,** and **y** sounds.

1. lluvia	6. pasillo	11. yogur
2. desarrollar	7. limón	12. estoy
3. animal	8. raya	13. taller
4. reciclar	9. resolver	14. hay
5. llegar	10. pantalla	15. mayor

2   **Oraciones** When you hear the number, read the corresponding sentence aloud. Then listen to the speaker and repeat the sentence.

1. Ayer por la mañana Leonor se lavó el pelo y se maquilló.
2. Ella tomó café con leche y desayunó pan con mantequilla.
3. Después su yerno vino a su casa para ayudarla.
4. Pero él se cayó en las escaleras del altillo y se lastimó la rodilla.
5. Leonor lo llevó al hospital.
6. Allí le dieron unas pastillas para el dolor.

3   **Refranes** Repeat each saying after the speaker to practice the **l, ll,** and **y** sounds.

1. Quien no oye consejo, no llega a viejo.[1]
2. A caballo regalado, no le mires el diente.[2]

4   **Dictado** You will hear five sentences. Each will be said twice. Listen carefully and write what you hear.

1. _____

2. _____

3. _____

4. _____

5. _____

He who doesn't listen to advice, doesn't reach old age. [1]
Don't look a gift horse in the mouth. [2]

estructura

13.1 The subjunctive with verbs of emotion

1 **Escoger** Listen to each statement and, in your lab manual, choose the most logical response.

1. a. Ojalá que se mejore pronto.
   b. Me alegro de que esté bien.

2. a. Espero que podamos ir a nadar mañana.
   b. Es una lástima que ya no lo podamos usar.

3. a. Me sorprende que venga temprano.
   b. Siento que se pierda la película.

4. a. Temo que el río esté contaminado.
   b. Me alegro de que vea bien.

5. a. Es ridículo que el gobierno controle cuando nos bañemos.
   b. Me gusta cepillarme los dientes.

6. a. Es triste que la gente cuide el césped.
   b. Me molesta que no hagamos nada para mejorar la situación.

2 **Transformar** Change each sentence you hear to the subjunctive mood using the expression in your lab manual. Repeat the correct answer after the speaker.

> **modelo**
> *You hear:* Cada año hay menos árboles en el mundo.
> *You see:* Es una lástima
> *You say:* Es una lástima que cada año haya menos árboles en el mundo.

1. Es triste
2. Es extraño
3. Es terrible
4. Es ridículo
5. Es una lástima
6. Me molesta

3 **Preguntas** Answer each question you hear using the cues in your lab manual. Repeat the correct response after the speaker.

> **modelo**
> *You hear:* ¿De qué tienes miedo?
> *You see:* nosotros / no resolver la crisis de energía
> *You say:* Tengo miedo de que nosotros no resolvamos la crisis de energía.

1. Ricardo / estudiar ecología
2. muchas personas / no preocuparse por el medio ambiente
3. tú / hacer un viaje a la selva
4. el gobierno / controlar el uso de la energía nuclear
5. los turistas / recoger las flores
6. haber / tantas plantas en el desierto

4 **El Club de Ecología** Listen to this conversation. Then read the statements in your lab manual and decide whether they are **cierto** or **falso**.

	Cierto	Falso
1. Carmen se alegra de que la presidenta del club empiece un programa de reciclaje.	○	○
2. Héctor espera que Carmen se enoje con la presidenta.	○	○
3. Carmen teme que los otros miembros (*members*) quieran limpiar las playas.	○	○
4. A Carmen le gusta ir a la playa.	○	○
5. A Héctor le sorprende que Carmen abandone (*resigns from*) el club.	○	○
6. Carmen cree que la presidenta va a cambiar de idea.	○	○

13.2 The subjunctive with doubt, disbelief, and denial

1 **Identificar** Listen to each sentence and decide whether you hear a verb in the indicative or the subjunctive in the subordinate clause. Mark an **X** in the appropriate column.

> **modelo**
>
> *You hear:* Creo que Nicolás va de excursión.
> *You mark:* an **X** under *indicative because you heard* **va**.

	indicative	subjunctive
Modelo	X	
1.		
2.		
3.		
4.		
5.		
6.		
7.		

2 **Cambiar** Change each sentence you hear to the negative. Repeat the correct answer after the speaker. *(7 items)*

> **modelo**
>
> Dudo que haga frío en Bogotá.
> **No dudo que hace frío en Bogotá.**

3 **Te ruego** Listen to this conversation between a father and daughter. Then choose the word or phrase in your lab manual that best completes each sentence.

1. Juanita quiere ir a la selva amazónica para . . .
   a. vivir con ls indios.   b. estudiar las aves tropicales.   c. estudiar las plantas tropicales.
2. Ella _____ que quiere ir.
   a. está segura de   b. no está segura de   c. niega
3. Su papá _____ que se enferme con malaria.
   a. está seguro   b. teme   c. niega
4. Juanita _____ que se enferme.
   a. duda   b. no duda   c. cree
5. _____ que el papá no quiera que ella vaya.
   a. Es cierto   b. No es cierto   c. No hay duda de
6. El papá dice que _____ que la selva amazónica es un lugar fantástico.
   a. es improbable   b. es imposible   c. no cabe duda de
7. _____ Juanita va a la selva amazónica.
   a. Es seguro que   b. Tal vez   c. No es probable que
8. Juanita _____ que su papá es el mejor papá del mundo.
   a. duda   b. no cree   c. cree

13.3 The subjunctive with conjunctions

1 **¿Lógico o ilógico?** You will hear some sentences. Decide if they are **lógico** or **ilógico**.

1. Lógico   Ilógico
2. Lógico   Ilógico
3. Lógico   Ilógico

4. Lógico   Ilógico
5. Lógico   Ilógico
6. Lógico   Ilógico

2 **A la entrada del parque** Listen to the park ranger's instructions. Then number the drawings in your lab manual in the correct order.

a.

b.

c.

d.

3 **Identificar** Listen to each sentence and mark an **X** in the appropriate column to indicate whether the subordinate clause expresses a future action, a habitual action, or a past action.

> **modelo**
>
> *You hear:* Voy a ir a caminar por el sendero tan pronto como llegues a casa.
> *You mark:* an **X** under *future action*.

	future action	habitual action	past action
Modelo	X		
1.			
2.			
3.			
4.			
5.			
6.			

vocabulario

You will now hear the vocabulary for **Lección 13** found on page 424 of your textbook. Listen and repeat each Spanish word or phrase after the speaker.

recursos
Lab CDs/MP3s
Lección 14

contextos

Lección 14

1 **¿Lógico o ilógico?** You will hear some questions and the responses. Decide if they are **lógico** or **ilógico**.

1. Lógico	Ilógico	3. Lógico	Ilógico	5. Lógico	Ilógico	7. Lógico	Ilógico
2. Lógico	Ilógico	4. Lógico	Ilógico	6. Lógico	Ilógico	8. Lógico	Ilógico

2 **Hacer diligencias** Look at the drawing in your lab manual and listen to Sofía's description of her day. During each pause, write the name of the place she went. The first one has been done for you.

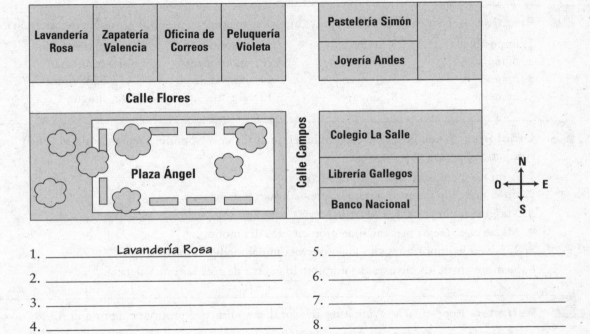

1. _____ Lavandería Rosa _____   5. _____

2. _____   6. _____

3. _____   7. _____

4. _____   8. _____

3 **Preguntas** Look once again at the drawing in activity 2 in your lab manual and answer each question you hear with the correct information. Repeat the correct response after the speaker. *(5 items)*

> **modelo**
> La joyería está al norte de la plaza, ¿verdad?
> No, la joyería *está* al *este* de la plaza.

4 **Perdidos en el centro** Listen to Carlos and Victoria's conversation and answer the questions in your lab manual.

1. ¿Qué buscan Carlos y Victoria? _____

2. ¿Quién les da la dirección? _____

3. ¿Qué deben hacer en el semáforo? _____

4. ¿A cuántas cuadras está del semáforo? _____

pronunciación

m and n

The letter **m** is pronounced like the *m* in the English word *made*.

    mamá   **m**arzo   **m**andar   **m**esa

The letter **n** is pronounced like the *n* in the English word *none*.

    norte   **n**adie   **n**unca   **n**ieto

When **n** is followed by the letter **v**, the **n** is pronounced like the Spanish **m**.

    e**nv**iar   i**nv**ierno   i**nv**itado   co**n V**íctor

1   **Práctica** Repeat each word or phrase after the speaker to practice pronouncing **m** and **n**.

1. imposible	5. número	9. enamorado	13. matrimonio
2. mañana	6. invitar	10. monumento	14. confirmar
3. mano	7. moreno	11. empleado	15. con Víctor
4. manejar	8. envase	12. encima	16. ningún

2   **Oraciones** When you hear each number, read the corresponding sentence aloud. Then listen to the speaker and repeat the sentence.

1. A mí no me gustan nada los mariscos.

2. En el mercado compro naranjas, melocotones y manzanas.

3. Mañana invito a Mario Martín a cenar conmigo.

4. Mario es el mejor mecánico de motocicletas del mundo.

5. También le importa mucho la conservación del medio ambiente.

6. Siempre envía los envases de aluminio al centro de reciclaje en Valencia.

3   **Refranes** Repeat each saying after the speaker to practice pronouncing **m** and **n**.

1. Más vale poco y bueno que mucho y malo. [1]

2. Mala hierba nunca muere. [2]

4   **Dictado** You will hear a paragraph. Listen carefully and write what you hear during the pauses. The entire paragraph will then be repeated so that you can check your work.

_____

_____

_____

_____

_____

_____

Quality is more important than quantity. [1]

Like a bad penny, it just keeps turning up. (lit. Bad grass never dies.) [2]

recursos

Lab CDs/MP3s
Lección 14

estructura

14.1 The subjunctive in adjective clauses

1 **Identificar** Listen to each statement or question. If it refers to a person, place, or thing that clearly exists or is known, mark an **X** in the **Sí** row. If it refers to a person, place, or thing that either does not exist or whose existence is uncertain, mark an **X** in the **No** row.

> **modelo**
>
> *You hear:* Buscamos un hotel que tenga piscina.
> *You mark:* an **X** in the **No** row because the existence of the hotel is uncertain.

	Modelo	1.	2.	3.	4.	5.	6.
Sí	_____	_____	_____	_____	_____	_____	_____
No	X	_____	_____	_____	_____	_____	_____

2 **Escoger** You will hear some sentences with a beep in place of the verb. Decide which verb best completes each sentence and circle it.

> **modelo**
>
> *You hear:* Tengo una cuenta corriente que *(beep)* gratis.
> *You circle:* **es** because the existence of the **cuenta corriente** is not in doubt.

1. tiene tenga   2. vende venda   3. vende venda   4. hacen hagan

3 **Cambiar** Change each sentence you hear into the negative. Repeat the correct answer after the speaker. *(6 items)*

> **modelo**
>
> Hay un restaurante aquí que sirve comida venezolana.
> No hay ningún restaurante aquí que sirva comida venezolana.

4 **Buscando amistad** Read the ads for pen pals found in your lab manual. Then listen to the four recorded personal ads. In your lab manual, write the name of the person whose written ad best suits each recorded personal ad.

Nombre: Gustavo Carrasquillo
Dirección: Casilla 204, La Paz, Bolivia
Edad: 20 años
Pasatiempos: Ver películas en inglés, leer revistas de política, escalar montañas, esquiar y hacer amistad con jóvenes de todo el mundo. Me pueden escribir en inglés o alemán.

Nombre: Claudia Morales
Dirección: Calle 4–14, Guatemala, Guatemala
Edad: 18 años
Pasatiempos: Ir a conciertos de rock, escuchar la radio, ver películas extranjeras, mandar y recibir correo electrónico.

Nombre: Alicia Duque
Dirección: Avenida Gran Capitán 26, Córdoba, España
Edad: 18 años
Pasatiempos: Ir al cine, a fiestas, bailar, hablar por teléfono y escribir canciones de amor. Pueden escribirme en francés.

Nombre: Antonio Ávila
Dirección: Apartado Postal 3007, Panamá, Panamá

Edad: 21 años
Pasatiempos: Entre mis pasatiempos están escribir cartas a amigos de todas partes del mundo, escuchar la radio, practicar deportes y leer revistas.

Nombre: Rosalinda Guerrero
Dirección: Calle 408 #3, Hatillo, Puerto Rico
Edad: 19 años
Pasatiempos: Navegar por Internet, leer sobre política, ir a conciertos y visitar museos de arte.

1. _____   3. _____

2. _____   4. _____

14.2 Nosotros/as commands

1 **Identificar** Listen to each statement. Mark an **X** in the **Sí** row if it is a command. Mark an **X** in the **No** row if it is not.

> **modelo**
>
> *You hear:* Abramos la tienda.
> *You mark:* an **X** next to **Sí**.

	Modelo	1.	2.	3.	4.	5.	6.
Sí	X	___	___	___	___	___	___
No	___	___	___	___	___	___	___

2 **Cambiar** Change each sentence you hear to a **nosotros/as** command. Repeat the correct answer after the speaker. *(8 items)*

> **modelo**
>
> Vamos a visitar la Plaza Bolívar.
> Visitemos la Plaza Bolívar.

3 **Preguntas** Answer each question you hear negatively. Then make another suggestion using the cue in your lab manual and a **nosotros/as** command.

> **modelo**
>
> *You hear:* ¿Cocinamos esta noche?
> *You see:* comer en el Restaurante Cambur.
> *You say:* No, no cocinemos esta noche. Comamos en el Restaurante Cambur.

1. jugar a las cartas

2. esquiarla

3. ir a la biblioteca

4. limpiar el sótano

4 **¿Cierto o falso?** Listen to Manuel and Elisa's conversation. Then read the statements in your lab manual and decide whether they are **cierto** or **falso**.

	Cierto	Falso
1. Manuel está muy ocupado.	○	○
2. Manuel va a acompañar a Elisa a hacer diligencias.	○	○
3. Primero van a ir al correo para comprar sellos.	○	○
4. Elisa quiere primero depositar el cheque.	○	○
5. Manuel y Elisa van a comprar el postre antes de ir al banco.	○	○
6. Elisa sugiere cortarse el pelo de último.	○	○

14.3 Past participles used as adjectives

1   **Identificar**   Listen to each sentence and write the past participle that is being used as an adjective.

> **modelo**
>
> *You hear:* Los programas musicales son divertidos.
> *You write:* **divertidos**

1. _____   5. _____

2. _____   6. _____

3. _____   7. _____

4. _____   8. _____

2   **Preguntas**   It has been a very bad day. Answer each question using the cue in your lab manual. Repeat the correct response after the speaker.

> **modelo**
>
> *You hear:* ¿Dónde está el libro?
> *You see:* perder
> *You say:* El libro está perdido.

1. romper	3. divorciar	5. caer	7. abrir	9. vender
2. morir	4. gastar	6. comer	8. dañar	

3   **¿Cierto o falso?**   Look at the drawing in your lab manual and listen to each statement. Indicate whether each statement is **cierto** or **falso**.

                           Cierto Falso

1. ○   ○
2. ○   ○
3. ○   ○
4. ○   ○
5. ○   ○
6. ○   ○

vocabulario

You will now hear the vocabulary for **Lección 14** found on page 452 of your textbook. Listen and repeat each Spanish word or phrase after the speaker.

contextos

Lección 15

1 **Identificar** You will hear a series of words or phrases. Write the word or phrase that does not belong in each group.

1. _____   3. _____   5. _____

2. _____   4. _____   6. _____

2 **Describir** For each drawing, you will hear a brief description. Indicate whether it is **cierto** or **falso** according to what you see.

1.   Cierto   Falso

2.   Cierto   Falso

3.   Cierto   Falso

4.   Cierto   Falso

3 **A entrenarse** Listen as Marisela describes her new fitness program. Then list the activities she plans to do each day in your lab manual.

lunes: _____

martes: _____

miércoles: _____

jueves: _____

viernes: _____

sábado: _____

domingo: _____

pronunciación

ch and p

In Spanish, the letter **ch** is pronounced like the *ch* sound in *church* and *chair*.

| Co**ch**abamba | no**ch**e | mo**ch**ila | mu**ch**a**ch**o | que**ch**ua |

In English, the letter *p* at the beginning of a word is pronounced with a puff of air. In contrast, the Spanish **p** is pronounced without the puff of air. It is somewhat like the *p* sound in *spin*. To check your pronunciation, hold the palm of your hand in front of your mouth as you say the following words. If you are making the **p** sound correctly, you should not feel a puff of air.

| La **P**az | **p**eso | **p**iscina | a**p**urarse | **p**roteína |

1   **Práctica**   Repeat each word after the speaker, focusing on the **ch** and **p** sounds.

1. archivo	4. lechuga	7. pie	10. chuleta
2. derecha	5. preocupado	8. cuerpo	11. champiñón
3. chau	6. operación	9. computadora	12. leche

2   **Oraciones**   When you hear the number, read the corresponding sentence aloud. Then listen to the speaker and repeat the sentence.

1. A muchos chicos les gusta el chocolate.
2. Te prohibieron comer chuletas por el colesterol.
3. ¿Has comprado el champán para la fiesta?
4. Chela perdió el cheque antes de depositarlo.
5. Levanto pesas para perder peso.
6. ¿Me prestas el champú?

3   **Refranes**   Repeat each saying after the speaker to practice the **ch** and **p** sounds.

1. Del dicho al hecho, hay mucho trecho. [1]
2. A perro flaco todo son pulgas. [2]

4   **Dictado**   You will hear eight sentences. Each will be said twice. Listen carefully and write what you hear.

1. _____
2. _____
3. _____
4. _____
5. _____
6. _____
7. _____
8. _____

It's easier said than done. [1]
It never rains, but it pours. [2]

recursos

Lab CDs/MP3s
Lección 15

estructura

15.1 The present perfect

1 **Identificar** Listen to each statement and mark an **X** in the column for the subject of the verb.

> **modelo**
> *You hear:* Nunca han hecho ejercicios aeróbicos.
> *You mark:* an **X** under **ellos.**

	yo	tú	él	nosotros	ellos
					X
Modelo	_____	_____	_____	_____	_____
1.	_____	_____	_____	_____	_____
2.	_____	_____	_____	_____	_____
3.	_____	_____	_____	_____	_____
4.	_____	_____	_____	_____	_____
5.	_____	_____	_____	_____	_____
6.	_____	_____	_____	_____	_____

2 **Transformar** Change each sentence you hear from the present indicative to the present perfect indicative. Repeat the correct answer after the speaker. *(8 items)*

> **modelo**
> Pedro y Ernesto salen del gimnasio.
> Pedro y Ernesto han salido del gimnasio.

3 **Preguntas** Answer each question you hear using the cue in your lab manual. Repeat the correct response after the speaker.

> **modelo**
> *You hear:* ¿Ha adelgazado Miguel?
> *You see:* sí / un poco
> *You say:* Sí, Miguel ha adelgazado un poco.

1. sí   3. no   5. no
2. sí   4. sí   6. no / todavía

4 **Consejos de una amiga** Listen to this conversation between Eva and Manuel. Then choose the correct ending for each statement in your lab manual.

1. Ellos están hablando de...
   a. que fumar es malo.   b. la salud de Manuel.   c. los problemas con sus clases.
2. Manuel dice que sufre presiones cuando...
   a. tiene exámenes.   b. hace gimnasia.   c. no puede dormir y fuma mucho.
3. Eva dice que ella...
   a. estudia durante el día. b. ha estudiado poco.   c. también está nerviosa.
4. Eva le dice a Manuel que...
   a. deje de fumar.   b. estudie más.   c. ellos pueden estudiar juntos.

15.2 The past perfect

1 **¿Lógico o ilógico?** You will hear some brief conversations. Indicate if they are **lógico** or **ilógico**.

1. Lógico	Ilógico	3. Lógico	Ilógico	5. Lógico	Ilógico
2. Lógico	Ilógico	4. Lógico	Ilógico	6. Lógico	Ilógico

2 **Transformar** Change each sentence you hear from the preterite to the past perfect indicative. Repeat the correct answer after the speaker. *(6 items)*

> **modelo**
> Marta nunca sufrió muchas presiones.
> Marta nunca había sufrido muchas presiones.

3 **Describir** Using the cues in your lab manual, describe what you and your friends had already done before your parents arrived for a visit. Repeat the correct answer after the speaker.

> **modelo**
> *You see:* preparar la cena
> *You hear:* mis amigas
> *You say:* Mis amigas ya habían preparado la cena.

1. limpiar el baño y la sala
2. sacar la basura
3. sacudir los muebles
4. poner la mesa
5. hacer las camas
6. darle de comer al gato

4 **Completar** Listen to this conversation and write the missing words in your lab manual. Then answer the questions.

JORGE ¡Hola, chico! Ayer vi a Carmen y no me lo podía creer, me dijo que te (1) _____

(2) _____ en el gimnasio. ¡Tú, que siempre

(3) _____ (4) _____ tan sedentario! ¿Es cierto?

RUBÉN Pues, sí. (5) _____ mucho de peso y me dolían las rodillas. Hacía

dos años que el médico me (6) _____ que tenía que mantenerme

en forma. Y finalmente, hace cuatro meses, decidí hacer gimnasia casi todos los días.

JORGE Te felicito (*I congratulate*), amigo. Yo también (7) _____

hace un año a hacer gimnasia. ¿Qué días vas? Quizás nos podemos encontrar allí.

RUBÉN (8) _____ todos los días al salir del trabajo. ¿Y tú? ¿Vas con Carmen?

JORGE Siempre (9) _____ juntos hasta que compré mi propio carro.

Ahora voy cuando quiero. Pero la semana que viene voy a tratar de ir después del trabajo para

verte por allí.

10. ¿Por qué es extraño que Rubén esté en el gimnasio?

_____

11. ¿Qué le había dicho el médico a Rubén?

_____

12. ¿Por qué no va Jorge con Carmen al gimnasio?

_____

15.3 The present perfect subjunctive

1   **Identificar**   Listen to each sentence and decide whether you hear a verb in the present perfect indicative, the past perfect indicative, or the present perfect subjunctive.

1. a. present perfect   b. past perfect   c. present perfect subjunctive
2. a. present perfect   b. past perfect   c. present perfect subjunctive
3. a. present perfect   b. past perfect   c. present perfect subjunctive
4. a. present perfect   b. past perfect   c. present perfect subjunctive
5. a. present perfect   b. past perfect   c. present perfect subjunctive
6. a. present perfect   b. past perfect   c. present perfect subjunctive
7. a. present perfect   b. past perfect   c. present perfect subjunctive
8. a. present perfect   b. past perfect   c. present perfect subjunctive

2   **Completar**   Complete each sentence you hear using the cue in your lab manual and the present perfect subjunctive. Repeat the correct response after the speaker.

> **modelo**
> *You see:* usted / llegar muy tarde
> *You hear:* Temo que...
> *You say:* **Temo que usted haya llegado muy tarde.**

1. ella / estar enferma
2. tú / dejar de fumar
3. ellos / salir de casa ya
4. nosotros / entrenarnos lo suficiente
5. él / ir al gimnasio
6. yo / casarme

3   **En el Gimnasio Cosmos**   Listen to this conversation between Eduardo and a personal trainer, then complete the form in your lab manual.

```
GIMNASIO COSMOS
Tel. 52-9023
Datos del cliente
Nombre: _____
Edad: _____
¿Cuándo fue la última vez que hizo ejercicio?
_____

¿Qué tipo de vida ha llevado últimamente, activa o pasiva?
_____

¿Consume alcohol?
_____

¿Fuma o ha fumado alguna vez?
```

vocabulario

You will now hear the vocabulary for **Lección 15** found on page 480 of your textbook. Listen and repeat each Spanish word or phrase after the speaker.

contextos

1 **Identificar** Listen to each description and then complete the sentence by identifying the person's occupation.

> **modelo**
>
> *You hear:* La Sra. Ortiz enseña a los estudiantes. Ella es...
> *You write:* maestra.

1. _____   3. _____   5. _____

2. _____   4. _____   6. _____

2 **Anuncios clasificados** Look at the ads and and listen to each statement. Then decide if the statement is **cierto** or **falso**.

EMPRESA INTERNACIONAL
Busca
CONTADOR

Requisitos:
• Tengan estudios de adminis-
  tración de empresas
• Hable español e inglés

Se ofrece:
• Horario flexible
• Salario semanal de 700
  córdobas
• Posibilidades de ascenso

Contacto: Sr. Flores
Tel: 492 2043

SE BUSCA DISEÑADOR
• Se ofrece un salario anual de 250.000
  córdobas.
• Excelentes beneficios
• Debe tener cinco años de experiencia.

Si está interesado, envíe currículum a
EMPRESA LÓPEZ
Fax 342 2396

	Cierto	Falso			Cierto	Falso			Cierto	Falso
1.	○	○		3.	○	○		5.	○	○
2.	○	○		4.	○	○		6.	○	○

3 **Publicidad** Listen to this radio advertisement and answer the questions in your lab manual.

1. ¿Qué tipo de empresa es Mano a Obra?

_____

2. ¿Qué hace esta empresa?

_____

3. ¿Cuál es la ocupación del Sr. Mendoza?

_____

4. ¿Qué le va a dar la empresa al Sr. Mendoza en un año?

_____

5. ¿En qué profesiones se especializa (*specializes*) Mano a Obra?

_____

recursos

Lab CDs/MP3s
Lección 16

pronunciación

Intonation

Intonation refers to the rise and fall in the pitch of a person's voice when speaking. Intonation patterns in Spanish are not the same as those in English, and they vary according to the type of sentence.

In normal statements, the pitch usually rises on the first stressed syllable.

A **mí** me ofrecieron un ascenso.   **Ca**da aspirante debe entregar una solicitud.

In exclamations, the pitch goes up on the first stressed syllable.

¡Oja**lá** venga!   ¡**Cla**ro que sí!

In questions with yes or no answers, the pitch rises to the highest level on the last stressed syllable.

¿Trajiste el cu**rrí**culum?   ¿Es usted arqui**tec**to?

In questions that request information, the pitch is highest on the stressed syllable of the interrogative word.

¿**Cuán**do renunciaste al trabajo?   ¿**Cuál** es su número de teléfono?

---

1   **Práctica**   Repeat each sentence after the speaker, imitating the intonation.

1. ¿Vas a venir a la reunión?   4. Estoy buscando un nuevo trabajo.
2. ¿Dónde trabajaba anteriormente?   5. Quiero cambiar de profesión.
3. ¡Qué difícil!   6. ¿Te interesa el puesto?

---

2   **Oraciones**   When you hear the number, say the speaker's lines in this dialogue aloud. Then listen to the speaker and repeat the sentences.

1. **REPARTIDOR (MOVER)** Trabajo para la Compañía de Transportes Alba. ¿Es usted el nuevo jefe?
2. **JEFE** Sí. ¿Qué desea?
3. **REPARTIDOR** Aquí le traigo los muebles de oficina. ¿Dónde quiere que ponga el escritorio?
4. **JEFE** Allí delante, debajo de la ventana. ¡Tenga cuidado! ¿Quiere romper la computadora?
5. **REPARTIDOR** ¡Perdón! Ya es tarde y estoy muy cansado.
6. **JEFE** Perdone usted, yo estoy muy nervioso. Hoy es mi primer día en el trabajo.

---

3   **Dictado**   You will hear a phone conversation. Listen carefully and write what you hear during the pauses. The entire conversation will then be repeated so that you can check your work.

PACO _____

_____

ISABEL _____

_____

PACO _____

_____

ISABEL _____

_____

PACO _____

_____

estructura

16.1 The future

1 Identificar Listen to each sentence and mark an **X** in the column for the subject of the verb.

> **modelo**
> You hear: Iré a la reunión.
> You mark: an **X** under **yo**.

	yo	tú	ella	nosotros	ustedes
Modelo	X				
1.					
2.					
3.					
4.					
5.					
6.					
7.					
8.					

2 Cambiar Change each sentence you hear to the future tense. Repeat the correct answer after the speaker. *(8 items)*

> **modelo**
> Ellos van a salir pronto.
> Ellos saldrán pronto.

3 Preguntas Answer each question you hear using the cues in your lab manual. Repeat the correct response after the speaker.

> **modelo**
> You hear: ¿Con quién saldrás esta noche?
> You see: Javier
> You say: Yo saldré con Javier.

1. no / nada
2. el lunes por la mañana
3. Santo Domingo
4. esta noche
5. 2:00 P.M.
6. sí
7. de periodista
8. la próxima semana

4 Nos mudamos Listen to this conversation between Fernando and Marisol. Then read the statements in your lab manual and decide whether they are **cierto** or **falso**.

	Cierto	Falso
1. Marisol y Emilio se mudarán a Granada.	○	○
2. Ellos saben cuándo se mudan.	○	○
3. Marisol y Emilio harán una excursión a la selva y las playas antes de que él empiece su nuevo trabajo.	○	○
4. Fernando no podrá visitarlos en Nicaragua en un futuro próximo.	○	○

16.2 The future perfect

1 **¿Lógico o ilógico?** You will hear some brief conversations. Indicate if they are **lógico** or **ilógico**.

	Lógico	Ilógico			Lógico	Ilógico
1.	○	○		5.	○	○
2.	○	○		6.	○	○
3.	○	○		7.	○	○
4.	○	○		8.	○	○

2 **Cambiar** Change each sentence from the future to the future perfect. Repeat the correct response after the speaker. *(8 items)*

> *modelo*
> Yo ganaré un millón de dólares.
> *Yo habré ganado un millón de dólares.*

3 **Preguntas** Look at the time line, which shows future events in Sofía's life, and answer each question you hear. Then repeat the correct response after the speaker.

> *modelo*
> *You hear:* ¿Qué habrá hecho Sofía en el año 2005?
> *You see:* 2005 / graduarse
> *You circle:* En el año 2005 Sofía se habrá graduado.

2005	2006	2010	2011	2014	2040
graduarse	encontrar trabajo	casarse	comprar casa	tener un hijo	jubilarse

4 **Planes futuros** Listen to this conversation between Germán and Vivian. Then choose the correct answer for each question in your lab manual.

1. ¿Qué va a pasar dentro de un mes?
   a. Se habrá acabado el semestre.
   b. Germán se habrá puesto nervioso.

2. ¿Qué habrá hecho el novio de Vivian?
   a. Se habrá ido de viaje.
   b. Habrá hecho las reservaciones.

3. Normalmente, ¿qué hace Germán durante las vacaciones?
   a. Él trabaja en la empresa de su familia.
   b. Él se va a Santo Domingo.

4. ¿Qué puesto habrá conseguido Germán dentro de dos años?
   a. Él será jefe de arquitectos.
   b. Él será gerente de un banco.

5. ¿Por qué dice Vivian que Germán no debe pensar tanto en el futuro?
   a. Porque ahora necesita preocuparse por los exámenes.
   b. Porque en el futuro no tendrá tiempo para ir de vacaciones.

16.3 The past subjunctive

1 **Identificar** Listen to the following verbs. Mark **Sí** if the verb is in the past subjunctive and **No** if it is in another tense.

1.	Sí	No	7.	Sí	No
2.	Sí	No	8.	Sí	No
3.	Sí	No	9.	Sí	No
4.	Sí	No	10.	Sí	No
5.	Sí	No	11.	Sí	No
6.	Sí	No	12.	Sí	No

2 **Cambiar** Form a new sentence using the cue you hear. Repeat the correct answer after the speaker. *(8 items)*

> modelo
>
> Marisa quería que yo dejara el trabajo. (mi hermana)
> Marisa quería que mi hermana *dejara el trabajo.*

3 **Completar** Complete each phrase you hear using the cue in your lab manual and the past subjunctive. Repeat the correct response after the speaker.

> modelo
>
> *You hear:* Esperábamos que tú...
> *You see:* seguir otra carrera
> *You say:* Esperábamos que tú siguieras otra carrera.

1. ir a renunciar al puesto
2. darte el aumento
3. invertir en su empresa
4. saber la verdad
5. poner un anuncio en los periódicos
6. llegar temprano al trabajo
7. ofrecerles mejores beneficios
8. gastar menos dinero

4 **El mundo de los negocios** Listen to this conversation between two coworkers and answer the questions in your lab manual.

1. ¿Qué le pidió el jefe a Elisa cuando la llamó por teléfono?

_____

2. ¿Qué le pidió el jefe a la empleada cuando entró (*entered*) en su oficina?

_____

3. ¿Qué le preguntó el jefe a Elisa?

_____

4. ¿Qué le contestó Elisa?

_____

vocabulario

You will now hear the vocabulary for **Lección 16** found on page 510 of your textbook. Listen and repeat each Spanish word or phrase after the speaker.

recursos
Lab CDs/MP3s
Lección 17

contextos

Lección 17

1   **Describir** For each drawing, you will hear a description. Decide whether it is **cierto** or **falso**.

1. Cierto   Falso   2. Cierto   Falso   3. Cierto   Falso

4. Cierto   Falso   5. Cierto   Falso   6. Cierto   Falso

2   **Identificar** You will hear four brief conversations. Choose the word from the list that identifies what they are talking about or where they are.

1. _____   a. la orquesta

2. _____   b. el poema

                              c. el tejido

3. _____   d. la cerámica

4. _____   e. los dibujos animados

                              f. el concurso

3   **La programación** Listen to this announcement about this afternoon's TV programs. Then answer the questions in your lab manual.

1. ¿Qué canal ofrece estos programas?

_____

2. ¿Qué programa empieza a las cuatro de la tarde?

_____

3. ¿Qué tipo de programa es *De tú a tú*?

_____

4. ¿Quién es Juan Muñoz?

_____

5. ¿Qué tipo de película es *Corazón roto*?

_____

pronunciación

Syllabification

In Spanish, every syllable has only one vowel or diphthong. If a single consonant (including **ch**, **ll**, and **rr**) occurs between two vowels, the consonant begins a new syllable.

co-che   dra-ma   mu-si-cal   ma-qui-lla-je   pe-rro   to-car

When two strong vowels (**a, e, o**) occur together, they are separated into two syllables. Diphthongs are never divided into separate syllables unless there is a written accent mark on the **i** or **u,** which breaks the diphthong.

ar-te-sa-ní-a   ma-es-tro   his-to-ria   tra-ge-dia

If two consonants occur between vowels, they are divided into two syllables, except when the second consonant is **l** or **r.**

al-fom-bra   or-ques-ta   pu-bli-car   ro-mán-ti-co

If three or four consonants occur between vowels, they are separated into syllables between the second and third consonants unless one of the letters is followed by **l** or **r.**

e-jem-plo   ins-pec-tor   trans-por-te

---

1   **Práctica**   Listen to the following words and divide each into syllables using slashes.

1. e s c u l p i r	6. a c a m p a r	11. p o e s í a
2. c o n c i e r t o	7. p r e m i o	12. ó p e r a
3. i n s t r u m e n t o	8. a p l a u d i r	13. a b u r r i r s e
4. c o n c u r s o	9. b a i l a r í n	14. c a n t a n t e
5. e s t r e l l a	10. e x t r a n j e r a	15. e n t r a d a

---

2   **Refranes**   Repeat each saying after the speaker.

1. De músico, poeta y loco, todos tenemos un poco. [1]

2. Tener más hambre que un maestro. [2]

---

3   **Dictado**   You will hear a conversation. Listen carefully and write what you hear during the pauses. The entire conversation will then be repeated so that you can check your work.

RAMÓN _____

_____

CELIA _____

RAMÓN _____

_____

CELIA _____

_____

RAMÓN _____

We are all part musician, part poet, and part fool. [1]
To be as poor as a churchmouse. [2]

recursos

Lab CDs/MP3s
Lección 17

estructura

17.1 The conditional

1   **Identificar**   Listen to each sentence and decide whether you hear a verb in the future, the conditional, or the imperfect tense.

1. a. future   b. conditional   c. imperfect
2. a. future   b. conditional   c. imperfect
3. a. future   b. conditional   c. imperfect
4. a. future   b. conditional   c. imperfect
5. a. future   b. conditional   c. imperfect
6. a. future   b. conditional   c. imperfect
7. a. future   b. conditional   c. imperfect
8. a. future   b. conditional   c. imperfect
9. a. future   b. conditional   c. imperfect
10. a. future   b. conditional   c. imperfect

2   **Cambiar**   Form a new sentence replacing the **iba a** + *infinitive* construction with the corresponding verb in the conditional. Repeat the correct answer after the speaker. *(6 items)*

> *modelo*
>
> Andrea dijo que iba a tocar el piano.
> Andrea dijo que tocaría el piano.

3   **Entrevista**   You are considering taking a job as the director of a new soap opera, and a reporter wants to know what the new show would be like. Answer his questions using the cues in your lab manual. Then repeat the correct response after the speaker.

> *modelo*
>
> *You hear:* ¿Cómo se llamaría la telenovela?
> *You see:* **Amor eterno.**
> *You say:* Se llamaría **Amor eterno.**

1. 23
2. San Salvador
3. romántica
4. Hispania y Univisión
5. Sí / muchísimo
6. $500.000

4   **Una exposición (*A show*)**   Cristina is planning an exhibition for her art work. Listen to her ideas and then indicate whether the statements in your lab manual are **cierto** or **falso**.

	Cierto	Falso
1. La fiesta sería al aire libre.	○	○
2. Invitaría al director de una revista.	○	○
3. Sus amigos podrían llevar algo de comer y beber.	○	○
4. Sus compañeros de trabajo vendrían a la fiesta.	○	○
5. Presentaría las pinturas de su primo.	○	○
6. A Cristina le gustaría publicar un libro sobre su escultura.	○	○

17.2 The conditional perfect

1 **Identificar** Listen to each statement and mark an **X** in the column for the subject of the verb.

> **modelo**
> *You hear:* Habrían preferido ir al concierto.
> *You mark:* an **X** under **ellos**.

	yo	tú	él	nosotros	ellos
					X
Modelo	_____	_____	_____	_____	_____
1.	_____	_____	_____	_____	_____
2.	_____	_____	_____	_____	_____
3.	_____	_____	_____	_____	_____
4.	_____	_____	_____	_____	_____
5.	_____	_____	_____	_____	_____
6.	_____	_____	_____	_____	_____

2 **¿Lógico o ilógico?** You will hear six brief conversations. Indicate if they are **lógico** or **ilógico**.

1. Lógico   Ilógico
2. Lógico   Ilógico
3. Lógico   Ilógico

4. Lógico   Ilógico
5. Lógico   Ilógico
6. Lógico   Ilógico

3 **¿Qué habría pasado?** Look at the program for an art conference that was canceled at the last minute and answer the questions you hear. Repeat the correct response after the speaker.

15F

VI CONFERENCIA ANUAL SOBRE EL ARTE

PROGRAMA DEL DÍA (Martes, 24)

10:00   Café y pasteles para todos
10:15   Presentación de todos los artistas que participan en la conferencia

Conferencias

10:30   El mundo de la televisión: el futuro de los canales públicos. Presentada por Marisa Monleón.
11:00   La artesanía: expresión cultural de los pueblos. Presentada por Roberto González.
11:30   El cuento hispanoamericano. Presentada por Mercedes Román.
12:00   Las canciones populares como formas poéticas. Presentada por Federico Martínez.
12:30   Las bellas artes en El Salvador. Presentada por Francisco Ruiz.

Espectáculos

4:00   Concierto de la Orquesta Tegucigalpa.
5:00   Lectura de poesía hondureña, por el Renato Lafuente

17.3 The past perfect subjunctive

1 **Identificar** Listen to each sentence and decide whether you hear a verb in the conditional, the conditional perfect, or the past perfect subjunctive tense in the subordinate clause.

1. a. conditional   b. conditional perfect   c. past perfect subjunctive
2. a. conditional   b. conditional perfect   c. past perfect subjunctive
3. a. conditional   b. conditional perfect   c. past perfect subjunctive
4. a. conditional   b. conditional perfect   c. past perfect subjunctive
5. a. conditional   b. conditional perfect   c. past perfect subjunctive
6. a. conditional   b. conditional perfect   c. past perfect subjunctive

2 **Escoger** You will hear some sentences with a beep in place of the verb. Decide which verb should complete each sentence and circle it.

> **modelo**
> You hear: Yo dudaba que él (*beep*) un buen actor
> You circle: **hubiera sido** *because the sentence is*
> **Yo dudaba que él hubiera sido un buen actor.**

1. había vivido   hubiera vivido   5. había empezado   hubiera empezado
2. habíamos bailado   hubiéramos bailado   6. habías estado   hubieras estado
3. había trabajado   hubiera trabajado   7. había conocido   hubiera conocido
4. habías dicho   hubieras dicho   8. había bebido   hubiera bebido

3 **Cambiar** Say that you didn't believe what these people had done using the past perfect subjunctive and the cues you hear. Repeat the correct answer after the speaker. *(7 items)*

> **modelo**
> Martín / ver el documental
> **No creía que Martín hubiera visto el documental.**

4 **Hoy en el cine** Listen to this talk show and answer the questions in your lab manual.

1. ¿Creyó Olivia que Óscar había ido a la fiesta?

_____

2. ¿Era cierto que Óscar había sido invitado a la fiesta?

_____

3. ¿Creía Óscar que José Santiago había hecho bien el papel de malo en *Acción final*?

_____

4. ¿Cómo habría tenido más éxito la película *El profesor*?

_____

vocabulario

You will now hear the vocabulary for **Lección 17** found on page 540 of your textbook. Listen and repeat each Spanish word or phrase after the speaker.

recursos

Lab CDs/MP3s
Lección 18

contextos

Lección 18

1 **Definiciones** You will hear some definitions. Write the letter of the word being defined.

1. _____   a. el terremoto
2. _____   b. el impuesto
3. _____   c. la tormenta
4. _____   d. la paz
5. _____   e. la guerra
6. _____   f. el tornado
7. _____   g. la encuesta
8. _____   h. las noticias

2 **¿Lógico o ilógico?** Listen to each news item and indicate if it is **lógico** or **ilógico**.

1. Lógico   Ilógico   5. Lógico   Ilógico
2. Lógico   Ilógico   6. Lógico   Ilógico
3. Lógico   Ilógico   7. Lógico   Ilógico
4. Lógico   Ilógico

3 **Describir** Look at the drawing and write the answer to each question you hear.

1. _____
2. _____
3. _____
4. _____

recursos

Lab CDs/MP3s
Lección 18

pronunciación

Review of word stress and accentuation

In Lesson 4, you learned that an accent mark is required when a word ends in a vowel, **n** or **s,** and the stress does *not* fall on the next to last syllable.

pren-sa   ar-**tí**-cu-lo   ca-**fé**   hu-ra-**cán**   **pú**-bli-co

If a word ends in any consonant other than **n** or **s,** and the stress does *not* fall on the last syllable, it requires an accent mark.

de-**ber**   a-**zú**-car   **cés**-ped   **fá**-cil   **mó**-dem

Accent marks are also used in Spanish to distinguish the meaning of one word from another. This is especially important for verbs where the stress often determines the tense and person.

el *(the)*   él *(he)*   mi *(my)*   mí *(me)*   tu *(your)*   tú *(you)*

compro *(I buy)* compró *(he bought)*   pague *(Ud. command)*   pagué *(I paid)*

1 **Práctica** Repeat each word after the speaker and add an accent mark where necessary.

1. contaminacion
2. policia
3. voto
4. ejercito
5. declaro
6. dificil
7. rapido
8. sofa
9. todavia
10. opera
11. arbol
12. luche

2 **Oraciones** When you hear the number, read the corresponding sentence aloud, focusing on the word stress. Then listen to the speaker and repeat the sentence.

1. Ramón Gómez informó ayer desde radio Bolívar que había peligro de inundación cerca del río Paraná.
2. Él explicó que toda la población necesitaba prepararse para cualquier cosa (*anything*) que pudiera ocurrir.
3. El ejército, ayudado de la policía, recorrió la región e informó a todos del peligro.

3 **Refranes** Repeat each saying after the speaker to practice word stress.

1. Quien perseveró, alcanzó. [1]
2. A fácil perdón, frecuente ladrón. [2]

4 **Dictado** You will hear a conversation. Listen carefully and write what you hear during the pauses. The entire conversation will be repeated so that you can check your work.

MERCEDES _____

ENRIQUE _____

MERCEDES _____

ENRIQUE _____

_____

MERCEDES _____

_____

He who perseveres, succeeds. [1]

Pardon one offense and you encourage many. [2]

estructura

18.1 Si clauses

1 **Escoger** You will hear some incomplete sentences. Choose the correct ending for each sentence.

1. a. llovía mucho.   b. lloviera mucho.
2. a. te gustó algún candidato.   b. te hubiera gustado algún candidato.
3. a. podemos ir de vacaciones juntos.   b. pudiéramos ir de vacaciones juntos.
4. a. el conductor hubiera tenido cuidado   b. el conductor habría tenido cuidado.
5. a. yo trabajaré con los pobres.   b. yo trabajaría con los pobres.
6. a. todos fuéramos ciudadanos responsables.   b. todos éramos cuidadanos responsables.
7. a. el presidente va a hablar esta tarde.   b. el presidente vaya a hablar esta tarde.
8. a. me lo pedirás.   b. me lo pidieras.
9. a. Eva sale con él.   b. Eva salga con él.
10. a. te habías comunicado con el dueño.   b. te hubieras comunicado con el dueño.

2 **Cambiar** Change each sentence from the future to the conditional. Repeat the correct answer after the speaker. *(6 items)*

> modelo
> Carlos se informará si escucha la radio.
> *Carlos se informaría si escuchara la radio.*

3 **Preguntas** Answer each question you hear using the cue in your lab manual. Repeat the correct response after the speaker.

> modelo
> *You hear:* ¿Qué harías si vieras un crimen?
> *You see:* llamar a la policía
> *You say:* Si yo viera un crimen, llamaría a la policía.

1. pedir un préstamo   3. buscar un trabajo nuevo   5. ir a Montevideo
2. ayudar a los pobres   4. quedarse en casa   6. hacer un viaje

4 **Un robo (*A break-in*)** Alicia and Fermín's house was burglarized. Listen to their conversation and answer the questions in your lab manual.

1. Según (*According to*) Fermín, ¿qué habría pasado si hubieran cerrado la puerta con llave?

_____

2. Según Alicia, ¿qué habría pasado si hubieran cerrado la puerta con llave?

_____

3. ¿Qué haría Alicia si tuvieran suficiente dinero?

_____

4. ¿Por qué se está poniendo nerviosa Alicia?

_____

18.2 Summary of the uses of the subjunctive

1 **Escoger** You will hear some incomplete sentences. Choose the correct ending for each sentence.

1. a. el terremoto había durado más de dos minutos.
   b. el terremoto durara más de dos minutos.
2. a. escribió sobre el incendio?
   b. escriba sobre el incendio?
3. a. no podían comunicarse con nosotros.
   b. no pudieran comunicarse con nosotros.
4. a. tenemos unos días de vacaciones.
   b. tengamos unos días de vacaciones.
5. a. los resultados de la encuesta están equivocados.
   b. los resultados de la encuesta estén equivocados.

6. a. ver el reportaje sobre el sexismo en los Estados Unidos.
   b. que ven el reportaje sobre el sexismo en los Estados Unidos.
7. a. te habrás enojado.
   b. te habrías enojado.
8. a. donde hay terremotos.
   b. donde haya habido terremotos.

2 **Transformar** Change each sentence you hear to the negative. Repeat the correct answer after the speaker. *(6 items)*

> **modelo**
> Creía que era muy peligroso.
> *No creía que fuera muy peligroso.*

3 **Preguntas** Answer each question you hear using the cue in your lab manual. Repeat the correct response after the speaker.

> **modelo**
> *You hear:* ¿Qué te pidió el jefe?
> *You see:* escribir los informes
> *You say:* El jefe me pidió que escribiera los informes.

1. hacer una encuesta de los votantes (*voters*)
2. mañana
3. tener experiencia
4. no
5. algunas personas no poder votar
6. los trabajadores no declararse en huelga

4 **El noticiero** Listen to this newscast. Then read the statements in your lab manual and indicate whether they are **cierto** or **falso**.

	Cierto	Falso
1. Roberto Carmona habló de los impuestos en su discurso.	○	○
2. No le sorprendió a nadie que Carmona anunciara que no se presentaría a las elecciones.	○	○
3. Corre el rumor de que Carmona está enfermo.	○	○
4. Inés espera que el Partido Liberal encuentre otro candidato pronto.	○	○
5. No creen que vayan a convocar (*to hold*) las elecciones en dos días.	○	○

vocabulario

You will now hear the vocabulary for **Lección 18** found on page 568 of your textbook. Listen and repeat each Spanish word or phrase after the speaker.